Then Along Came Barney:
The Story of a Dog Who Changed
My Mind About Pit Bulls

Barbara Bullington

Then Along Came Barney:
The Story of A Dog Who Changed
My Mind About Pit Bulls

Copyright © 2008 by Barbara Bullington

ISBN: 1440469156
EAN-13: 9781440469152

Also by the author:

After the Break,
The Work of Life (a novel)

For: Kevin (Did I mention you're my Pooh Bear?)

And: Jesse, Mom, Cicely, John

Also: Amanda (Your answers to my millions of questions about Barney were always so helpful and reassuring!)

Plus: Barney and the entire furry gang who inspired this book.

Finally: Last but not least, thank you to all those pit bull advocates and organizations out there who have worked so hard and continue to work to help dogs.

Author's Note: Some people and organizations don't like the term "dog owner" because it implies that a dog is property without feelings or the right to be treated ethically. I tried to avoid using the term throughout this book, except in rare instances when a better/more appropriate substitution given the circumstance described was lacking.

•

Chapter 1

It's true enough that pit bulls grab and hold on—but what they most often grab and refuse to let go of is your heart, not your arm.
                          —Vicki Hearne, "Bandit"

I love dogs. I mean, *really* love dogs. I live with six of the furry and drooling but loveable creatures.

But I don't want anymore.

I came to North Carolina in 2000 to teach at East Carolina University without any definitive plans as to my length of stay here. Then, last year, my sister and her husband became parents. Now, my five-year plan involves getting back up to New York where they live, and where I grew up, so I can be the doting aunt I always wanted to be.

I'm also 38 years old and happily single, too busy with work and other things for romance. But, what if I want to actually date a guy in the future?

So, I'm trying to cool it on the canines.

Okay, and the felines. I have 14 cats. Having a close friend who runs her own animal rescue organization contributed to that. For a while, anytime she had a hard-to-place cat, I was her "go-to" person (see "sucker").

Anyway, it's around 7 p.m. on a January evening. Even thought it's North Carolina, it is pretty darn cold outside. I'm moving from room to room, cleaning up, checking my email, doing laundry and engaging in various other after-work activities. The dogs won't stop barking. I keep checking the front door to see if someone's there until it occurs to me that this is the bark they usually use when there's an animal—often a deer or a rabbit— passing through our yard.

I go into the sunroom and am hit by a gust of cold air. I close the door to the kitchen behind me to keep the dogs inside. They all jump up and peer at me through the windows in that door. I open the front door. As if on cue, a brown and tan dog I've never seen before hobbles up the two concrete steps and into my sunroom.

There's something wrong with him. It's like he's bent into a C-shape with the top of his spine forming the curve of the C. My first thought is that someone must have been confining him in some kind of crate too small for his size. He's breathing loudly and grunting as he circles around in search of a place to lie down, which he does almost immediately on the carpet-covered base of the cat scratching post.

He's extremely thin. Sort of like one of those dog skeleton replicas in veterinary offices. His stomach is bloated though, and its barrel shape stands out in contrast to his visible ribs.

This knee-high visitor was unexpected to say the least, and I was hoping for a nice, quiet Wednesday evening of watching some television and going to bed. (It's early in the semester, so there isn't much grading to do yet.)

I can't bring him in past the sunroom because I don't want this stray to mingle with my dogs till I'm sure that he can't pass any parasites or anything else on to them. It's a definite possibility. Mixed in with his short fur, there are at least six very swollen ticks attached to his body.

Leaving him in the sunroom, I call the vet and am referred to the after-hours emergency center. They tell me to bring him in, but caution that they charge a flat $100 fee for emergency visits. Any treatment charges will be added onto that.

My home is out in the country. Actually, the house belongs to my sister and her husband. They own their own home on Long Island in New York, but wanted to invest in more property a couple of years back. I found this great three-acre home and they bought it. I live in it and take care of things. One of the benefits is that it's extremely scenic. One of the drawbacks is that it's a half-hour drive into town.

I also promised not to add any pets to my menagerie after moving in. So it was kind of awkward when they visited last year and were greeted by two more dogs than they expected. They didn't say anything, but I haven't pushed my luck since. I will try to help this little guy for now, but then I'm going to have to find him a home. After a quick assessment of his features, I don't think he's going to be an easy animal to place with a loving owner. His snout is short and his jaw round. An apparent pit bull.

Any scared or injured animal can be unpredictable in temperament. That he might be a pit bull enhances my trepidation. I don't know a lot about this type of dog, but, like everyone else, I've heard stories. What if picking him up causes him to bite out of fear or pain? It's doubtful that he's ever been on a leash or even worn a collar before, and now doesn't seem like the right time to try either. I pick up the largest cat carrier in my collection; it's kept in the sunroom for ease (I'm always taking one of the cats to the vet for something).

I place the carrier on the floor in front of him and open the door. He walks right in. Bingo! After closing the carrier and securing the latch, I load him into the car. It's doubtful he's ever been in a car before, and, on the ride into town, he howls like a hungry human infant. I sing songs to which I know most of the words—"The Star Spangled Banner," and "There's a Light" from "The Rocky Horror Picture Show." (Yes, it's an eclectic mix, but I think most people would be surprised if they tried it to learn how few songs to which they actually know all the words.) He settles down somewhat, but not a lot. No, this isn't how I planned for the evening to go.

The emergency veterinary hospital is having a slow night, so we get immediate attention.

"He's just a puppy," the veterinarian says, adding that the little guy appears to be about five and a half months old. He's also 23 pounds—10 pounds too light for his size. His colon is "blocked" and it's causing him pain—hence the hunched posture. They're going to need about an hour to administer an enema and deal with the results. The vet tells me I can go up the road to IHOP and get a coffee. I opt to go to my office, since campus is also nearby.

While waiting to return to the animal hospital, I try to figure out where this dog came from. Anyone could have dropped him off. Everyone knows I'm a "dog person." When my space heater caught on fire in my bedroom last winter and what seemed like the entire Stokes Fire Department responded, there were a lot of firefighters in my bedroom and on my lawn. They all saw and/or heard how many dogs I had.

Or, I could have made a random comment in the dog park to anyone that five out of six of my dogs came from animal shelters, and that I have a very soft spot in my heart for strays. Plus, most of my students have heard me tell the occasional funny pet story in class.

Yes, it could have been anyone.

But that still doesn't stop me from trying to figure out who it was.

I fear that the dog came from my next-door neighbors. The dog's condition kind of looks like their handiwork. They currently have at least four dogs in their backyard. Apparently, no one has ever told them there's been a new advancement in veterinary medicine, a quick little operation that can prevent dogs from reproducing and help prevent overpopulation. When I moved in, there were three beagle mixes tied up in their backyard about 50 yards from their trailer. Then, one of their dogs had puppies—a lot of puppies—and there were about 14 canines back there for a while in a constantly-growing metal fence-type pen. So far, all their dogs are beagles and hounds. "Hunting dogs." But they have a teenage son who is now old enough to drive and who is growing up in a culture that makes it cool for a teenage male to have a pit bull.

As someone who's been concerned about animal rights for years, I have a very hard time seeing eye to eye with these neighbors. So, I pray this dog is not theirs because there's no way I'd let them have him back. But, that leads to yet another problem with keeping him. I could never leave him in my yard unattended, in case he's a fugitive from Tetanus Land (my nickname for the collection of rusted metal objects they keep amassing in their backyard). If he was theirs, somehow got loose and made it over here, what if they tried to sneak over and take him back?

No, I definitely need to find this dog a home elsewhere.

Back at the vet's office, I watch as the assistant walks out with the stray wrapped in a blanket. She's holding him upside down with his back and neck cradled in her arms like he's a human infant. He looks so sweet and relaxed. He's actually very well sedated. She hands him over to me after I pay the bill —— $170 (not too bad—not great, but at least I don't need to be sedated too).

They tell me I can keep the blanket (both very kind of them and probably also because the enema is still working its magic a little) and I opt to let him sleep on it for the ride home. The assistant places him on the passenger seat while I stick the carrier in the back. She asks me hopefully if I plan to keep him.

"For the immediate future," I tell her. Sure, it would be a happy ending from her perspective if the lost, starving puppy ended up with the nice lady. The way he hobbled so purposely into my sunroom comes into my mind. It was almost as if he had reached his destination and was ready to rest. But, I can't keep him…Can I?

What am I thinking? I *can't* keep this animal. I'm going to nurse him back to health and find him a good home. On the ride to my house, he starts to stir, and, even though he's sedated, begins to howl again. This time, I'm too tired to sing.

At home, I first plan on him sleeping in the sunroom, since I can keep him separated from the rest of the animals out there. That plan goes out the window when I realize it's far too cold. I move him into the spare bedroom, which holds my old dresser and some boxes of odds and ends, and place some old blankets on the floor as a makeshift bed. I close the door and start to get ready for bed. All's pretty quiet until about 10:30 p.m. when my head hits the pillow. Suddenly, the howling starts back up. I go in and spend about an hour petting the puppy and trying to soothe him. When I leave the room, the noise begins again.

By midnight, his howls are loud and continuous. He's in a panic and his rear end can't be helping. Dirt and fur, along with other non-specified things, are coming out of his now unblocked tummy.

"What on earth have you been eating?" I ask him.

As far as I can tell without looking any closer than I have to, he may have ingested a very decomposed animal carcass out of complete desperation.

I call the emergency hospital. They tell me to come pick up some tranquilizers so that he'll settle down, hopefully stop pushing his bowels, and sleep. I wouldn't mind some sleep myself.

Libby, one of my larger dogs, comes with me for the ride back into town. The streets are practically empty, but, when I get stuck at lights next to other cars, I'm glad Libby is in the passenger seat. Bringing one of my big dogs on errands at night makes me feel safe, especially since a scary encounter once outside a video store when I'm pretty sure I would have ended up on a missing flyer in the post office if my Lab, Samantha, hadn't intervened. Her loud barks out of my car window at a stranger who was following me and asking odd questions managed to scare him away.

About an hour later, the puppy has swallowed a sedative. I get into my bed without looking at the clock—I don't even want to know the time. All is quiet, and, as I'm winding down and hoping to fall asleep quickly so I won't be too tired at work tomorrow (actually, today), I think about how to go about finding the little guy a home.

It's hard to place any kind of dog in a caring environment. Now, add on that he looks like a pit bull and that all kinds of negative stereotyping surrounds such dogs, and the options will likely decrease. Also, many people like to adopt cute, little puppies. This guy is at that stage when he's big enough that a lot of the cute puppy features are gone, but he still isn't fully grown enough to qualify as an adult—sort of like that awkward age child stars hit when their agents stop taking their calls.

I would never place an ad in the newspaper and take the risk that he might not end up in a good place. There's no way I'm going to give him to someone who would keep him outside all the time or otherwise not treat him right. He's been through too much already.

One of the last things I think before drifting off is that this dog could be living in my spare bedroom for some time to come.

Chapter 2

For the next three days, the puppy spends most of his time in the spare bedroom. He loves soft surfaces, including the decorative pillows stored in there, which he quickly claimed for his sleeping area (alas, none will survive the experience and will all have to be thrown out). This preference makes me once again curious about where he came from.

If someone dumped him off at my house they must have cared enough to get him somewhere he might be safe. But a dog with so many ticks couldn't possibly have been an indoor animal. Did he get lost and somehow end up on my doorstep? Would roaming with no access to regular meals account for the unhealthy weight? I have a hard time believing that could be the answer.

The houses on this long, winding country road are spaced far apart for the most part. Many are separated by fields and patches of woods. Across from my house is a field, so I have no neighbors on that side of the street. There's the trailer on Tetanus Land next door to my house on the left and woods next to them. On the other side of my property is a very nicely kept ranch-type home. A family lives there. They're not animal people—something I found out when my dog, Casey, got loose and decided to run into their yard. The father and preteen son started yelling "git! git!" (Southern for "Get out of here dog!") as loud as they could.

Beyond them are three more houses I pass when walking my dogs. I don't know the people in those houses. I hear barking and see movement, but the homes are too far from the road for me to be able to tell what kinds of dogs live there. I never really paid attention. If the puppy didn't come from those residences, and I don't think he did, he would have had to walk a long way to get here. People drive up and down this country road at breakneck speeds; it's hard to believe that he could have walked from anywhere without getting hit by a vehicle. Besides, the veterinarian had to trim the puppy's nails when I brought him to the emergency animal hospital. If he'd been walking so much wouldn't his nails have been worn down?

Trying to figure out where he came from is probably futile, but it would be helpful to know so I can get some idea of how he got so sick. The vet has given me antibiotics to give the pup once a day, along with de-worming medication, and an over-the-counter diarrhea medication.

He's in no shape to go anywhere else in the house. Since the enema opened up the floodgates, so to speak, the puppy has been an almost nonstop dispenser of diarrhea. I covered the spare bedroom floor with newspapers, which I find myself replacing about three to four times a day. The blanket I put down for him and the once very lovely green and red decorative pillows need frequent washing too. It's not a pretty picture.

With the exception of the howling the night he came, he's been quiet. When I close the bedroom door after feeding or visiting him, he doesn't whine or whimper. This silence is surprising to me. Except for Samantha, whom I adopted with my then-boyfriend when she was a puppy, I have taken in dogs over 9 months of age. For one, "teens" and adults are harder for shelters to place. But, unlike many people, I prefer dogs over puppies because, in theory at least, they don't whine as much or engage in as much destructive behavior (or at least not for as long). And they're often already housetrained or easier to housetrain.

But, with this puppy, there's a distinct lack of whining and chewing on furniture or valuables. He does get the hiccups a lot, and he snores. Beyond that, the most noise he makes is a grunting when he engages in anything of effort. It reminds me of the noises made by Yoda when Luke visited him in the swamp. It's also the kind of grumbling you might expect from an old man as opposed to a young dog. I email my friend and former student who has two pit bulls. She assures me this is a normal sound and that her dogs, Abby and Sheba, make it too.

I spend a lot of time looking at this dog. He is so different from my other canines. His snout is short and round, especially compared to my labs. When he chews on the rubber bones I've given him, his jaw opens and closes like a playful Venus flytrap.

There's a lot of personality wrapped up in this little dog package, so coming up with a good name is hard, but it's getting awkward referring to him as "hey you." It also seems like a good idea to give him a name that sounds appealing and non-threatening. This guy has enough disadvantages as a stray and a possible pit bull. Naming him something like Killer or Chaos is out. After fourteen cats and six dogs, I'm having trouble coming up with new monikers, so I ask my sister (who, being a very compassionate person, fortunately, isn't too upset about my latest furry boarder from a landlord standpoint). After some thought, she suggests Barney. It has an "ee" sound at the end, like my other dogs (even Samantha's nickname is Sammy). It fits him pretty well in general.

After about a week and a half, Barney has grown tired of the spare bedroom and gives me a look that would melt an iceberg whenever I leave the room. His stool is a little firmer, and he's almost finished with his antibiotics, so I decide to let him out into the rest of the house for a couple of hours at a time on a trial basis. All the rooms in the house have tile flooring, so I don't have to worry about carpet stains.

I do worry about my animals. Introducing a new pet into the mix can be tricky; it's hard to predict how the other animals will react to Barney and vice versa. Most of the cats get along with the dogs—they're all pretty used to each other. A few kitties are even very affectionate toward the dogs and will curl up next to them for a nap. But, one cat—Stella—hates dogs with a passion. Whenever one of my dogs tries to sniff her or steps into her own personal space, she'll hiss at them on her good days, claw at them on her bad. She once got a claw stuck in my Lab/shepherd, Libby's, face when Libby attempted an affectionate lick. So, I'm shocked when Barney walks right up to Stella and butts her nose with his. I'm about to intervene when Stella (a.k.a. The Dog Hater) rubs her chin on Barney's face. It's an unprecedented display of affection on her part, and I guess it gives Barney some self-confidence because he starts to try to engage the dogs in play.

But, with the exception of Libby, they're being wusses and rebuff him.

I'm surprised at my pack of six. Before I go any further, I should probably describe them and their personalities:

There's Samantha, my black Labrador retriever who turns 10 years old this year. I got her from a farm in Pennsylvania with my then-boyfriend, whom I lived with, along with my then preteen son, Kevin, when I was a graduate student. Sammy was my only dog for about four years, which is about two years longer than the boyfriend lasted.

On a whim, after I had been in North Carolina for about two years, I went to the Humane Society one day, and adopted a brown and white Corgi mix named Penny. That was in a February. I can still remember how diminutive and lost she looked in the pen, with her tall ears, long body and short legs. I had brought Samantha to see how she got along with a possible new brother or sister, and the two took to each other right away.

At the end of that year, I was going to the craft store to buy materials to make shelves using the Dremmel my mom gave me for Christmas. The craft store is located right next door to the pet store and the local animal shelter had dogs for adoption out front. I stopped "just to take a quick look" and pat some furry heads, and ended up adopting Casey, a 1-year-old sight hound/black Labrador. In spite of his long, stick figure legs and pencil thin body, Casey's face reminded me too much of Samantha for me to go home without him.

Maggy, a spitz mix, joined the rapidly expanding pack after I had been surfing the Internet and stumbled across the local animal shelter's Web site. When I actually saw her in the shelter, she was so scared of her surroundings and so timid that she wouldn't walk. I literally had to pick her shaking body up and carry out to my car. After time, she mellowed out. Her blond fur started to lengthen and get thicker. A cross between a Pomeranian and a golden retriever (that's my guess anyway), she's so beautiful that it took me a long time to get used to her without thinking, "What the heck are you doing with a bunch of mutts like the rest of us?"

That summer, I adopted Bella while volunteering at the pet store with a friend of mine who is the president and founder of a non-profit organization, the Marley Fund. We were there to help get cats adopted and to inform the public about preventing feline retroviruses, especially feline leukemia. The animal shelter volunteers also happened to be there with dogs that day. Bella was a small terrier mix and one of the most loving dogs in the world. Unfortunately, she passed away a year and a half later from a freak illness.

I had moved from town into the house in the country (yes, the one I promised not to bring any new animals into) and, soon after, ended up adopting a Bella look-alike named Lilly (a beagle/terrier mix) and a black Lab/German shepherd-mix named Libby. They were both slightly under a year old. They both came from the animal shelter. I had only gone in for one and couldn't leave without both of them.

While all except for Samantha have backgrounds of being abused, neglected or abandoned, they have become very comfortable with their new lives, perhaps even spoiled. They aren't exactly thrilled that there's an intruder. Libby is the only one who wants to be friends.

Casey, who is about 50 pounds, jumps onto the top of the back of the couch and stays perched up there whenever Barney tries to come near him. As the only male dog in the pack until now, Casey doesn't seem overjoyed to have another male for company.

Samantha is a bit of a loner and prefers to spend a lot of time in my bedroom. She gives the impression of finding the other dogs simply too immature and hyper to deal with.

Penny, who is usually pretty friendly with people and dogs, stays in the living room but still keeps her distance from Barney.

Lilly—who is such a sweet, little dog and who loves human attention—won't stop growling at Barney.

I guess maybe part of the problem is that it has been over two years since I've introduced a new pet into the household. Or, maybe they secretly read the newspapers and have heard bad things about pit bulls. Or, do they want to go to New York and, thus, worry about the possibility of setbacks to my five-year plan to get there?

Barney continues to be a trooper by playing with Libby and trying to befriend the others. He's doing better in general until a few days later—a Sunday afternoon. He sits on the couch without much movement. His head feels like a space heater set on high. This is also the first time I've been unable to get him to eat. He even turns away from the extra-costly canned food, and then the cooked chicken breast I make a special trip to the store to get.

It's really worrisome. I don't want to put him through the stress of another emergency hospital trip but decide that, in the morning, I will take him to the regular vet's office (which isn't open on Sundays). Later, having tried rice to no avail, as a last-ditched effort, I leave some cooked grits in a bowl in the spare bedroom and go into my room to try to get some sleep.

The next morning, I'm afraid to open the door to Barney's room. I still haven't recovered from Bella's death. I can't take another loss.

Remarkably, the bowl of grits is empty and Barney is standing up, bright-eyed and wagging his tail. He jumps up and puts his paws on my thighs to greet me. From that moment on, I think of grits as miracle food. I even cook some more for myself to increase my own energy.

The relief I feel after Barney's recovery makes me realize that I've become much more attached to this dog than I planned. I've also been thinking a lot about how much he has changed my mind about pit bulls. This is a dog who almost starved to death, and yet, he has no food aggression with my other dogs or cats. If he's eating and any other animal comes near him, it doesn't faze him. No growling, no change of posture. This lack of aggression is an excellent sign.

None of my dogs has ever exhibited food aggression towards me. One of the golden rules about pets my parents taught me when I was young was that animals are unpredictable, so you should never push your luck. So, I don't stick my hand in the food bin (they have one large bin instead of many regular-sized bowls) or otherwise interrupt them when they're eating, no matter how much I doubt they might react negatively. Why take chances? But, they do sometimes get aggressive toward each other.

If Lilly is eating and anyone attempts to eat anywhere near her at the same time, she'll growl. Libby will go a step further and sometimes lunge at the other dogs. They all kind of take turns eating throughout the day. I don't know what happened to Libby in her past that she learned to guard her food like that, but it's something I've been hoping she'll grow out of.

Anyway, I'm starting to become skeptical of the pit bull reputation. This particular dog is more of a floppy, fun-loving, furry sweetheart than a menace to society, and I want other people to know. It is somewhat strange that I feel this way—I mean, of all people, how did I end up wanting to be an ambassador for the pit bull world? For the past two weeks, I've referred to Barney in my emails to family and friends as a *pitt bull*—maybe because I live in Pitt County. It's not until I do a search on Amazon.com for books on caring for this kind of dog that I realize it should be *pit bull*. Spelling errors aside, what else do I know, or not know, about these dogs?

Each semester, in my Media Writing class(es), I tell my students about cultivation theory—the idea that our world view is shaped by what we see in the media. Putting that theory to the test now, I think of my prior exposure to and knowledge of pit bulls:

I recall that one of my son's favorite rappers a few years back had a video that was often on MTV. The rapper likened himself to a pit bull—fierce, tenacious, unstoppable. If I'm recalling it correctly, images of a pit straining against a chain to get at the camera were interspersed with shots of the rapper.

I also remember a book I read by Jonathan Katz. In "The New Work of Dogs," Katz explores various dog owners and the lives of their dogs. I remember the saddest part of the book was his description of a boy who beat his pit bull with a wood board to toughen it up before walks through the neighborhood.

I recall seeing an episode of "Animal Precinct" on Animal Planet, in which a drug addict kept a pit bull as a pet in the abandoned building in which she lived and, during the day, wheeled the dog around in a stroller like a baby. The only way the animal control officers could get the frightened dog to come with them out of the building was by pushing it in the stroller. Various bits and pieces of other episodes of that show come to mind, even though it would be preferable to forget the many incidents of the ASPCA responding to reports of abandoned and starving pit bulls or other dogs horribly injured in dog fights.

Then, there are other bits and pieces—sort of a grab bag of media exposure. I remember hearing news reports over the years about pits that attacked and maimed innocent children or adults. I vaguely recall that Petey on "The Little Rascals" reruns I grew up watching might have been a pit bull. The videos on "America's Funniest Home Videos," and similar shows, in which dogs grab hold of ropes and are swung around by the strength of their jaws, are probably of pits.

Then, there's also some very limited personal experience. Maybe a week or two before Barney showed up, I was at the neighborhood dog park one day (a very frequent hangout for me) when a male dog, probably about 50 pounds, that I think was a pit, jumped up on my lap while I was sitting on the bench watching my dogs run around. (By the way, I only take two to four dogs at a time to the dog park because bringing all of them at once would be crazy, possibly even suicidal.) At the time, I remember thinking that the dog was just a big, sweet baby dressed up in a scary dog costume.

I also think of a friend and former student who has two pit bulls. I haven't seen her dogs in person, but love the picture she sent me via email of the two of them sleeping in the classic spoon position with what looked like grins on their faces.

And there's no getting around it; I've had a long-running debate with my son. When he was a teenager, he would constantly ask for a pit bull puppy and I would tell him that such a dog probably wouldn't get along well with the cats. He responded that, like any dog, pit bulls could either be raised to be ferocious or friendly. He said it depended on the dog, not the owner. I definitely saw his point, but I still couldn't get those images from those news reports out of my head. Why take chances with a pit when other dog breeds had such better reputations? That was my stance. I have to eat a lot of crow when my now 21-year-old son phones me and I tell him what's going on.

And that's part of the problem with media cultivation—the image the media gives us of something is not always accurate or complete. Sometimes the only way to find out the truth about something is to experience it directly.

In the coming days, Barney starts to perk up. I let him into the backyard with Libby one day. When I come back from the bathroom, I look out the window and catch a glimpse of the two of them playing chase. This is the first time I've seen him run! Then Libby offers him the end of her rope toy and they engage in a game of tug of war. It's heartwarming to see him romping like any other dog.

His stomach continues to be a mess though. In spite of following the veterinarian's orders and giving Barney rice and other binding foods, I find that he still alternates between passing something that somewhat resembles typical dog feces and diarrhea. I've resorted to keeping the entire living room and kitchen floors covered with newspaper. It's sort of like living in a giant bird cage. I let him into the backyard constantly, but still I'm cleaning up an awful lot of his messes inside the house.

I keep an eye on Barney for any signs of relapse into illness besides his stomach troubles. The first time I see him sleeping with his head hanging off the couch, it scares the heck out of me. His neck—which usually appears short, but stretched out is actually quite long—is hanging down and his eyes are kind of rolled back in his head. I fear he's having a seizure or something until I realize this is merely a comfortable sleeping position.

I don't hear him bark until he's lived with me for about a month. It's a high-pitched noise that sounds a lot like a child plunking the high keys on a piano. His bark is usually to get the attention of me or the dogs or cats. It's a playful sound and accompanying it is his body language, which involves wiggles, jumps and lots of rapid tail wagging. Even though he is still mostly rebuked or ignored in his attempts to get the other animals to play with him, he remains as tenacious and stubborn as a, well…you know. And, when that doesn't work, he'll do this kind of flying leap onto one of the stuffed dog toys scattered about the living room and play by himself.

He's also starting to fill out, although he's still thin for his sturdy frame. His ears, which would be about two and a half inches high if they stood up completely, fold over endearingly at half their height. His fur, which was so short and thin when he first limped into my sunroom, (although still short) is becoming thicker and the white is turning shiny and bright—when light hits it, it glows like sun on snow.

He snoozes at my feet as I work on the computer at the desk in the kitchen or sits next to me when I work on my laptop on the couch. He loves to be nearby, which is endearing, yet slightly problematic given that he is still very gassy and that the gas is potent to say the least. It can be difficult to answer emails when tears are streaming down my face and I'm trying not to gag.

I want to start socializing him soon, but decide to wait until his stomach is in better shape before a trip into town. In the meantime, I ask my friend, Amanda, about her pit bulls. She tells me that she seriously doesn't think there has been a time when she's gone in public with her two pits when people didn't act scared of her dogs or otherwise behave in a way that was unwarranted.

One time, she and her husband took them to PetSmart.

"I think it was their first time, so they were all excited and each time we went down a row people scattered," she related, adding that one man grabbed his children and fled to another aisle. (In the coming months, I'll read and hear similar comments from numerous people who have experienced almost the same kind of reaction to their pits in public.)

"If all these people who acted terrified of these dogs came to my house and just spent some time with them, they'd have a complete change of heart," Amanda said. "My dad did, I have a few friends (who) did and I always tell people to come see my dogs and see for themselves. They are, by far, the sweetest dogs I've ever had."

Unfortunately, not even everyone in her own family has embraced her "children."

"I bought my very first house last year and my family never visits me, except for my dad on occasion and the reason is because of my dogs," she said. "And, at every family event, someone brings up some random dog attack involving pit bulls and…shoves it in my face every time."

My family tolerates *my* pets. My sister and mom are animal people too—my mom can't visit me without constantly worrying about her cat back in New York, and my sister feeds stray cats among many, many acts of kindness toward large and small animals.

But what about strangers? Am I ready to deal with the type of behavior Amanda described when I bring

Barney out in public? I already have a low tolerance for people who don't like dogs. (Believe me, there are reasons, which I'll get into later on.)

On the other hand, when I ask myself if I'm ready to give this guy up, there's no doubt he has grown on me. Even now, as I type in my laptop, he's curled up on the couch by my side and snoring. It scares me how protective I feel of him.

In other words, while I can't actually bring myself to say that I'm keeping him, I can't say the opposite either.

Chapter 3

Because there's no doubt Barney is working his way into my heart, it starts to seem like a good idea to learn more about pit bulls.

On a Sunday, I go onto campus and surf the Internet in my office (much faster than my dial-up connection at home). A site called The Real Pit Bull (www.realpitbull.com) notes that there's no such thing as too much research if you're considering adopting such a dog.

I agree it is good advice to research any dog breed before adoption. If more people were educated about dog behavior in general and more aware of breed-specific traits, exercise needs, and so forth, there would likely be fewer people abandoning dogs that surprise, disappoint or overwhelm with unexpected behavior. I'm obviously doing this in reverse, but better late than never, I guess.

Still, I do believe that breed descriptions can be broad generalizations with exceptions. After I adopted my Corgi mix, Penny, I was so stupefied by what a wonderful overall dog she was (affectionate but determined to keep up with the bigger dogs, the only dog to actually jump right into the bathtub when it was time for a bath, etc.) that I became curious about the breed. I remember reading at the time that Corgis can be very dominant and not get along well with other canines. Penny is extremely friendly to dogs and cats. She's great with people too, kids included. At the dog park, I've seen her run over to comfort a little girl who was frightened after another dog ran into and knocked her over. Penny acted more maternal than the girl's mother, who never put down her cell phone. On that same visit, when two dogs got into a minor spat, Penny ran over to try to serve as peacemaker.

If Penny could speak, her first words would be, "Why can't we all just get along? Take me to the Middle East—It's time to straighten out all that silliness over there." Her next words would be, "Can you give me something to eat and then take me swimming?" (Although she loves water, I once had one of those supernatural strength experiences you hear about, like a mom lifting a car off her toddler. In my case is was lifting a wet 60-pound Corgi mix—yes, she's huge for a Corgi—out of the lake with one arm while balancing on a floating dock; she was panicking after she realized she couldn't touch the bottom of the deep part of the lake she had just jumped into.)

I read on. The site also states that pit bulls are "very aggressive toward other dogs and small animals."

This doesn't sound like Barney.

I read on.

"If you are the type who likes to have a dog that will mingle peacefully with other dogs, visit the off-leash dog park, etc., the pit bull is not for you." The site also ominously warns, "Never leave a pit bull unattended with other animals."

Real Pit Bull further relates that pit bulls are "high-energy." That doesn't bother me too much. It's not as if my other dogs are exactly slugs. On any given day, none of them would choose a nap over a walk, unless perhaps it was raining. (Remarkably—even though none came from posh backgrounds, some living outdoors in the past—they don't like to go out in the rain.) When Sammy was younger, she would chase a Frisbee for an hour and follow that with a swim in the lake. When Maggy gets excited, she tends to stand up on her hind legs and jump as if she's auditioning for a circus act. Lilly, my terrier mix, runs from room to room till her tongue is hanging out…High energy I can handle.

Another important consideration noted at this site and others is that there are locations that have laws preventing or restricting pit bull ownership. While a number of cities have outright bans on ownership with steep fines for violation, other regulations require a certain leash length, muzzling in public, purchase of liability insurance or special housing requirements. Some insurance companies will deny homeowner coverage if there is a pit bull on the property. Sheesh! Something else to check into.

At www.understand-a-bull.com, I find a link for pit bull laws or proposed legislation by state. My county has neither according to this site, but some North Carolina counties and towns are discussing the possibilities of introducing legislation. The closest one listed is Roanoke Rapids, which is only about an hour and a half from where I live.

I don't want to stay in my office too long. Samantha and Libby are waiting in the car to go to the nearby dog park. I print out the rest of the information from the site and some from a few others, and take it all with me.

At the fenced-in dog park, I release Samantha and Libby from their leashes. They both take off, frolicking in different directions. I find a bench to settle on, and continue reading the printed out pages.

"Dog-aggression in pit bulls may not show itself to full extent until the animal reaches maturity (usually after 2). With puppies, you never quite know how dog-aggressive they'll be as adults."

That's also from Real Pit Bull and, so far, it's the scariest thing I've read. Could it be true? Could Barney be a big, loveable clown now, but suddenly turn into a bloodthirsty demon the day of his second birthday? I love my other animals very much. The thought of any harm coming to them makes me queasy. Especially if it's me who puts them in harm's way. To be fair, the site does make the comments about age and temperament in relation to the topic of dog adoption and the argument for adopting an adult pit instead of a puppy. The site's advice for those getting a pit bull for the first time but worried about other dogs in the household is to get a dog around 3 years old, as a "dog of this age has manifested, for the most part, his true temperament and personality…He's very much 'what you see is what you get'."

It might sound like a writer's device or a movie plot development so predictable and convenient that it's corny, but at almost the precise moment I've read this information and really start to feel doubt about Barney's stability, a brown and white pit bull wearing a pink collar runs by playing a friendly game of chase with another dog. Fierce? Scary? At the moment, a goldfish might seem a more aggressive pet than this carefree canine.

I take a look around. There are about 15 dogs in the park right now, an average number for a Sunday afternoon. Out of the 15, there are two that appear to be pits. The other one is white and almost as big as my black Lab, Samantha. I watch as Libby, Samantha and this white pit engage in a group sniff and my apprehension continues to melt away.

Okay, I'm pretty certain, but not a hundred percent sure those dogs are pits, pit mixes or some kind of dog similar in appearance, which makes me realize that the question I should address next is: *What exactly is a pit bull?*

The Understand-a-bull (think about the name for a minute—it's pretty clever) Web site notes that pit bull is not a breed of dog. The term is actually used for three breeds: the American Pit Bull Terrier, the American Staffordshire Terrier and the Staffordshire Bull Terrier. This site was founded by someone who had pit bulls as family pets for about eight years and then found herself in a fight to keep her dogs when breed specific legislation was passed where she lived. She posted the site to educate others.

A test at this Web site shows pictures of over 20 dogs and asks which is the pit bull. While almost all might be identified by some as pits, only one actually belongs in that category. (When I try my hand at the test online later, I fail miserably at identifying the true pit.)

Also noteworthy at this site, which is full of additional great information, is a chart that lists the average number of people in America killed every year by certain causes. Cigarettes—at 440,000—are at the top of the list of killers. Pit bulls are at the very bottom—with 3. Yet, the more research I do, the more I find that there are a lot of myths about pit bulls out there and many innocent dogs suffering because of unnecessary fear generated as a result.

Back at home, I look up the three breeds from Understand-a-bull in a well-worn breed book. Barney definitely has some similar traits. He's got the same medium-sized feet with the same short, white, pointy nails. He has the broad shoulders and short fur, and is bow-legged. He also has black spots on his skin that show through his fur, just like the dogs in the pictures. It's harder to tell about other traits because he still hasn't filled out to an average weight and isn't fully grown.

So far I'm learning a lot and not deterred from keeping Barney, but not only do I want to make sure he's right for my home – if I were to keep him, which I'm not saying I'm going to, I'm just thinking about it – I also want to make sure that *I* would be good for *him*.

I do a Google search for online tests that help people select the type of dog that would be most appropriate for them. There are a lot of these kinds of tests on the Internet.

At www.dogbreedinfo.com, questions are about capacity for basic animal care (including whether I live in an apartment or home and the size of my backyard), as well as walking and grooming regularity preferences. The search yields 19 breeds, including standard and toy poodles, and the small and delightfully unusual-looking Chinese Crested (picture a Chihuahua with a Farrah Fawcett hairstyle). The pit bull breeds are nowhere on the list.

Another test, this one on SelectSmart.com, covers many areas of preference, including dog appearance, ease of training and temperament. Out of the 10 results shown for me, poodle is once again a contender, likely because I expressed that I do have slight allergies (poodles have hypoallergenic fur). Labrador retriever is also on the list – a good thing, given that I have three Labs.

When taking these tests, I specify that the results should only include breeds as opposed to possible mixes. It's not that I personally care about breed—I don't understand why breeders continue to help create litters of animals and charge for them when there are plenty of great animals already out there in need of homes—but because I want to get more clear-cut results for this little experiment.

I could probably take a lot more of these tests and none of the pit bull breeds would be in my top 10, or even top 50. Which brings me to my next question: What kind of personality should a pit bull owner have?

The Pit Bull Rescue Central Web site describes pit bulls as having superior mental characteristics. Barney did learn to come to me when I said "come" pretty quickly, but sometimes he looks at me blankly when I ask him to do something simple such as "get down" off the couch so I can adjust the couch cover.

Over the years, I have read a lot about different types of dog breeds. Border collies, for example, are fascinating because of their drive, unbridled energy and preference for spending time occupied with work. (Which is again a generalization—a couple of months ago, I met a woman with a rare border collie who pretty much liked to snooze at people's feet all day long.) I've read a few very interesting books about people who have adopted border collies and the related adventures. I also often use my breed guide at home for reference. Almost every breed description I read, no matter what the source, includes a sentence or two about how intelligent the breed is. It could be a collie, a Corgi, a Lab, etc. They're all "intelligent" dogs. I would like to know if there are any breeds that are characterized as being particularly stupid or not too bright. If there are, it seems no one wants to admit to it.

Intelligence is not necessarily number one on my list of preferences in a dog, although it's nice when dogs pick up commands quickly or can adapt well to varying situations. Yet, at the end of the day, they're dogs. It's not like I need them to do my taxes or something.

Anyway, the Rescue site also notes that people should be aware that pit bulls can be determined dogs. Barney does seem to possess this trait. He's a barrel-ahead kind of guy. If he wants to sit on the couch, he'll climb up and make himself comfortable—regardless of whether there's room. If another cat or dog is in the place he's going for, he'll simply climb right on top of them or me. Even though he does this in a non-menacing way, it isn't a trait that helps make him anymore popular around here than he is already with the other animals.

A few days later, I ask Angela Parker, the manager and co-owner of Top Dog Academy in Greenville, about her experience with pit bulls and she says that they can be the most difficult types of dogs to train because they are such dominant animals. She also states problems can arise when a person has a pit bull as a puppy and lets it run rampant because it's cute, only to be greatly surprised and afraid when the pit bull gets older and growls or nips the first time it doesn't get its way.

High energy, intelligence and determination sounds like a somewhat challenging combination. And, indeed, my friend Amanda describes her pit bulls not only as "angels," but as in need of "lots of exercise and training." She adopted Abby as a puppy first, and later took in Sheba.

"They have their issues but we spend hours and hours each week working with them and trying to make them social, friendly girls," she says. "These are dogs you can't just chain up and ignore. They need attention to function well in the world. The reason Sheba has some slight aggression issues is because of the way she was raised as a puppy. She didn't get that constant attention that Abby got as a puppy. Sheba still needs some work but she's such a better dog now than before we got her."

Like I said earlier, I can deal with high energy, but I do wonder what types of activity dogs like Barney would most benefit from.

The book "Pit Bulls for Dummies" recommends lots of toys, especially hard rubber balls (that are at least large enough they can't be swallowed) or even a partially deflated soccer ball. The book also mentions that pit bulls can do well in competitive activities, including weight pulling, agility training and tracking (requiring a dog to track a scent along a trail).

Many think of pit bulls fighting when they hear of these dogs, which, obviously, helps give them their bad reputation. To me, organized fights are disgusting. They're also illegal in all 50 states and a felony in almost all states according to the Humane Society of the United States.

By the way, I'm not exploring the dog fighting topic too much for this book. Although their connection to dog fighting is obviously relevant to a discussion of pit bulls, I don't have the stomach to do an in depth investigative look into the dog fighting underworld. I have a hard time merely watching videos or even seeing pictures of dogs being abused in this way. From the information I have seen, those who make the argument that these dogs fight because they want to, thus making dog fighting a violent but natural "sport," should be aware that the dogs—both the winners and losers—are treated deplorably by humans in between fights. Web sites, such as Diane's Jessups's Pit Bull Informational Pages, do provide more information about dog fighting. I also come across a number of Web sites and articles describing how former fighting dogs can be rehabilitated as family pets if careful temperament testing is done to make sure the dog is a good candidate. For some heartwarming writing about this topic and other pit bull-related stories/comments, visit hubpages.com/hub/Pit_Bull_Rehabilitation. (Yes, it's a long Web site, but I think it's worth the trouble of typing it in to read some of the pro-pit articles posted there.) In this book, I'd prefer to focus on how pit bulls with no apparent history of being fought can be great family pets. And Barney is my particular focus.

Anyway, weight pulling, on the other hand, is something I've never heard of before. But, the more I read, the more I come across weight pulling mentioned as an activity for pits. Weight pulling is done on snow, dirt or rail. In the rail competitions, a cart with wheels is involved and dogs pull up to thousands of pounds in competition with other dogs. In some competitions, baiting is allowed. Baiting means that a toy or some other object is used to entice the dog forward. Dogs are given a set amount of time during which they must pull the weight.

Weight pulling is not something I would likely ever engage Barney in, but I check to see what people are saying about it online in related chat rooms. On the negative side, some think that it's cruel to the dog. Others believe that pulling competitions are a way for those who fight dogs to connect with each other. As for the positive, some comment that as long as the dog isn't forced to pull too much weight, it's good exercise and enjoyable for the dog.

My dogs' main form of exercising is walking, or running around at the dog park or in my backyard. They don't undergo much formal training, although there are some exceptions. About six months after I adopted Casey, I had been having so many problems with him that, when I won four weeks of training by a local dog trainer (by placing the winning bid at a charity auction for a training package valued at $500), I was ecstatic.

Other than that, I do teach my dogs basic commands, such as "come," "stay" (which they even listen to sometimes), and "get down." They are housetrained too. But, I'm not too big on the whole training at home thing. Although I think some dog rescuers would disagree with my thinking, and I understand why, my gut feeling when I adopted everyone but Samantha was that these dogs had suffered abuse or neglect or abandonment, or all of the above, so now it was their time to take it easy and live the good life. (Before anyone writes me a letter telling me how wrong I am, don't worry, I change my mind by the end of this book.)

Plus, getting them used to living indoors has been a challenge in itself. Maggy, for example, spent the first six months with me chewing and destroying any book she could get her paws on. I had to keep placing my books on the next shelf up because she kept reaching higher than I anticipated. I'd come home daily to find a book cover full of teeth marks and various pages strewn throughout the house. I was forced to buy the local library a brand new copy of a historical novel about tapestry making (about as exciting as it sounds, although, surprisingly, some gratuitous sex) after Maggy somehow got a hold of the checked out copy off the table, which is at least twice as tall as she is.

Libby has been the most difficult out of any dog I've taken in. This lab/shepherd mix was a challenge from day one. In public, she's a different dog. People always describe her as "really sweet," including the veterinarians who have given her shots, and the workers at the kennel where she spent a couple of my vacations. (My other dogs stayed home, and I had someone come in to feed them and let them out.)

At home, Libby has all kinds of issues, including the food aggression I mentioned earlier. There was also a lot of destruction in her early days. When I first adopted her, she chewed giant chunks out of my mattress while I was washing the sheets. One night, under the cover of darkness, she somehow pulled the plug of the air conditioner out of the outlet and chewed her way through it. We then spent a very hot night trying to get back to sleep without AC.

In the coming months, she also chewed through the cords of the following: at least two vacuum cleaners, two carpet cleaners, one five-foot-tall indoor decorative fountain valued at $200, a computer monitor, an air filter, a lamp, an electric staple/nail gun, and my son's lava lamp.

She also completely chewed apart the seat part of a new reclining lawn chair, all of an antique rocking chair that I had restored a couple of months earlier, and the phone part of a brand new phone/answering machine combo. Some of the decorative pillows I used to have on the couch in the living room were shredded (the reason the rest ended up in the spare room where Barney finished them off), as were a few pillows from my bed. Those are only some of the highlights. Don't even get me started on the number of remote controls she went through.

You might wonder why I let things go that far; for example, why not make sure all cords were out of reach? The answer is that she is sneaky! I would leave the vacuum for maybe a minute if nature called thinking it was safe as weeks had passed without any cord chewing incidents. I would come back from the bathroom to the vacuum cleaner and its newly severed cord. She also managed to get into things I thought were safely stored away in cabinets (which, as it turned out, she can open, along with the refrigerator and screen door). The phone was put on the counter after taking it out of the box. I left the room to do something and, when I came back, she was happily chewing on the receiver. The phone battery got damaged in the process, and I was never able to use that phone for anything more than a 10-minute call before the power would cut off.

After awhile, the more expenses incurred replacing things she had ruined, the more I realized I was in too deep to give up on this dog. I also tried to make sure she had plenty of chew toys— something that worked well with the other dogs (except for Maggy, who doesn't like to chew anything but paper and cardboard). She went through these very quickly and then went right back to the remote controls.

Libby's destructive streak has diminished somewhat in the two years since she was adopted. And she *does* also have a "really sweet" side. And she *is* the only dog who has shown affection toward Barney so far.

I guess my point is that research and previous experiences with other dogs can be helpful; but every dog is different and you just never know what will be the correct combination of training and exercise for that particular animal.

For more advice, I've been looking to the few autobiographies by people who have developed relationships with pit bulls (or pit bull "types"). In the book "Bandit," animal trainer Vicki Hearne (who passed away from lung cancer in 2001) talked about how in 1988 she saved a dog. The animal had been incorrectly identified as a pit bull (Bandit was one of the bulldog breeds but not a pit) from being put to sleep. The dog was on his own property and bit in defense of his owner. Bandit later bit again – this time it was his owner he bit. The owner had been hitting him. Bandit was impounded and Hearne stepped in to fight against the dog's death sentence.

One of the most comforting paragraphs for me from the entire book is the following: "The claim about the Jekyll-Hyde syndrome is, like all the popular ideas about pit bulls, baloney. There is no such thing as the dog discussed in the press and in the courtrooms, and I am not the kind of writer who would lie to you about a thing like that. There exist dangerous dogs. There exist dogs who are not wrapped tight. In particular, there exist fear biters. And there exist a few, a very very very few, dogs who will go for just about anyone. I knew one dog—one dog—who liked to bite people and who didn't straighten out after the owner put a lot of effort into training him, using the Koehler method. That dog, Liberty was his name, was definitely bad news. He was a Malamute."

It's reassuring to read the words of a such an advocate, but it's disheartening to know that, as far back as the 1980s, pit bulls were having their reputations maligned. Hearne also pointed out that before the pit bull, the Doberman was the dog to fear. I remember that. When I was growing up on Long Island in the 1970s and the 1980s, the fear of Dobermans was rampant. They were the dog of choice for the "tough guys" and those who wanted dogs to guard "important" things, such as drugs or a lot full of rusty cars.

I remember a friend of mine, Heather, telling me how she stopped on her way to school each day to sneak food through a fence to a few Dobermans kept in a junkyard and used as watchdogs. We were in the eighth grade. Like a lot of people, the owners of the junkyard must have believed that the best way to make a dog a good watchdog was to not feed it much or give it any attention. Believe me, that would make me mean, so I'm sure it works for some dogs. Anyway, I remember being impressed by Heather and rethinking my attitude toward

Dobermans. If the ones she was feeding on the sly were actually as benign as she said, maybe others weren't so bad.

Sometime in the 1990s, the Doberman quietly slipped from the top of the scary dog list. Nowadays, at the dog park people don't even look twice at these dogs (except for me when one peed on my dog, Samantha). Maybe junkyard owners started figuring out they couldn't trust dogs that let 13-year-old girls feed them Doritos.

After about a month and a half since Barney arrived, I *do* now know a whole lot more than I did about pit bulls. His stomach is improving. Hopefully, he can soon be brought into public to start socializing with strangers (both people and animals). What I don't know is what will happen on these outings. What will we experience from other people? Will we be ostracized? Embraced? Ignored? Maybe all three? All I can do is hope the rest of the world sees what I do: A sweet, strong, friendly, funny, sometimes stubborn, little guy with boundless energy and a desire to fit in.

Or more simply put: A sheep in wolf's clothing.

Chapter 4

Barney's first trip out in public since the one to the emergency animal hospital turns out to be yet another visit to the veterinarian. Even after almost two months, his stomach has still not recovered from his days of deprivation. He makes a noise whenever he goes to the bathroom. It's loud and very upsetting to hear; he's been through enough – more pain doesn't seem fair.

The veterinarian notices that Barney looks over his shoulder to make sure that I'm following him into the examination room.

"It's okay, she's coming too," she tells Barney.

His faith in and trust of me tugs at my heart. This veterinarian likes dogs and doesn't appear the least bit afraid of Barney. I tell her about the noise Barney makes when going to the bathroom, describing it as "a horrible yelping." Confirming my description, Barney has an accident of the number two kind on the floor while the vet is running tests for parasites. Hearing Barney "scream," she rushes back into the room.

"Is *that* the noise!?" she asks, her eyes wide with surprise. (When my son—who has watched "Jurassic Park" numerous times— heard it over the phone one day he asked, "Did you just adopt a velociraptor?")

She then prescribes a "really strong" antibiotic and sends me home with a bunch of other medications, asking me to bring Barney back in 10 days for a follow-up. I can't have him neutered until his diarrhea clears up and she wants to hold off on his vaccinations until our next visit. Thus, Barney will need to continue to spend all of his time at home; trips to the dog park and elsewhere are postponed.

Even with these problems, Barney is so full of energy and becoming such a good-looking compact mass of muscle that I can't wait to take him out in public and show him off. I do continue to be somewhat apprehensive, especially because now that I'm paying attention I'm hearing pit bull stories all over the place.

I watch a "Saturday Night Live" re-run. Actually, the television is on as background noise while I work on this chapter. A Jimmy Fallon joke on a Weekend Update segment catches my attention. Fallon relates that, in New York, someone started a campaign to rename the pit bull. Hoping to change the bad reputation of these dogs, the campaign was focused on getting people to call them "New Yorkies." Fallon's punch-line was: Now when a pit bull is eating your child's face, you can call it a New Yorkie.

For work, I attend a journalism conference about news coverage of health insurance-related issues. It's held at UNC-Chapel Hill. You'd think this topic would be about as far removed from dogs as you can get, but a lawyer on the panel tells a story about two pit bulls who allegedly "broke into" an animal shelter and killed a number of animals inside, including a couple of cats. Everyone in the room, except me, clucks knowingly, as in, "Oh yeah, pit bulls. What do you expect?"

With all due respect to the lawyer, it does make for a very dramatic story, but I think of Barney nuzzling my cats, and I wonder how much of it is actually true. Afterwards, I think about contacting the lawyer but I'm not sure there's any way I can ask him to verify some of the details without sounding as if I doubt his veracity. Instead, I do a search on the Internet to look for information about the event, and the closest report I can find is an article about a man who broke into that particular animal shelter to *steal some pit bulls*. That sounds a little more realistic. I can't picture a bunch of dogs circling an animal shelter thinking to themselves, "Man, we gotta get in there where all the terrified barking is, instead of out here enjoying our freedom. Oh, and while we're in there, let's kill some cats just for the heck of it."

The following week, I'm getting my hair cut and Jenna—a petite, extremely thin woman in her 20s, who has cut my hair for a few years now—tells me fond stories about her two pit bulls and how funny they are playing together. Like my friend, Amanda, also noted about her two pits, Jenna tells me that hers are very sensitive. She says one actually turned his head away from her after she gave him a bath as if to indicate, "How could you do that to me? I smelled so good, and now I smell like a girl!"

I can identify with her dogs' flair for the dramatic. All my dogs sleep in my bedroom, but I haven't been able to let Barney in. Well…I broke down and let him in twice, and both times he pooped all over my comforter within the first five minutes. In spite of the accidents, the look he gives me when I shut the bedroom door each night as he stands in the hallway fills me with guilt.

Jenna then segues into describing an episode of "The People's Court" that she recently saw about how four pit bulls attacked and killed a poodle when it wandered into the backyard of the house where the pit bulls lived.

"If a poodle wandered into my yard, my dogs would eat it alive and there wouldn't be any evidence," she says nonchalantly as she snips my bangs and I try not to cringe.

Later on, back at home with much better-looking hair, I think more about what Jenna said. While the poodle story sounds horrible for sure, and while my heart goes out to any person whose pet is attacked, as well as the poor animal, I force myself to mentally set aside all the hysteria about pit bulls and think about it rationally for a second.

Suppose my dogs were in the backyard and a rabbit or other small animal came along. If I weren't there to supervise, I'm not entirely sure that creature would be welcomed as a friend and playmate. *Dinner* might be more likely to be on my dogs' minds. Another golden rule my parents told me about dogs is that animals can act very aggressively when strange animals or people enter their territory.

I also learned this firsthand a couple of times in my life. Once, when I was about 4 years old, my mom brought me to visit a friend of hers. The friend, an elderly woman, had a pet poodle that had just been groomed and was shut in the bedroom. I still remember the woman telling me that the dog hated to be groomed and was in a bad mood. I think she also said something about him not liking children. So, of course, once my mother and her friend became engaged in a conversation, I had to sneak down the hallway and, for some reason that is definitely not clear to me now, go into the room where the poodle was.

Pretty much what I remember next is a small yet fiercely barking flash of curly (albeit well groomed) fur and teeth coming at me. It didn't get close enough to bite me, but I was scared of dogs for quite some time. It took years before I liked small, yippy dogs, especially poodles, again.

Then, when I was about 7 or 8, I was at the house of a friend of mine. Her mother was out doing errands. They had a dog. I don't even recall what kind it was—possibly some kind of medium-sized terrier. My friend went to the bathroom and I remember not liking the way the dog was looking at me. The next thing I knew it was growling and charging. I ran into the parents' bedroom and closed the door. My friend's mother was chagrined when she came back and found out what happened. The dog was kept outside the house tied up in the yard after that. Although the incident was pretty scary, I felt really guilty about the dog losing its freedom—especially for doing what it thought was its job—that is, protecting its territory and the child in it.

Around that time, my father explained that if I ever came upon a stray or otherwise loose dog, the worst thing to do was to show fear. He said to ball up my hands in fists so the dog couldn't get a good hold if it tried to bite, and to slowly walk in the opposite direction. Having that knowledge made me feel much more in control when coming across canines in the future. Acting calmly was some of the very first language of how to communicate with dogs I learned. It not only prevented me from not disliking dogs, it gave me the confidence to befriend them.

Thank God for that because I have benefited so much from the relationships I've developed with canines, starting with a dog named Ajax whom a kind owner used to let me walk when my family lived at the beach one summer. That was years ago, but I still remember how exhilarating it felt to walk that huge, powerful dog (I was probably 9 and Ajax was a German shepherd mix.)

And there was also my love of Snoopy. My parents wouldn't let me and my sister have a dog of our own, but I would cuddle up with my Snoopy stuffed animal and wish it were a real dog. I'll talk more about that later—my relationship with dogs, not Snoopy—but what I'm working toward now is the idea that any dog can act aggressively. This would be especially true if someone entered its territory, or if it was on the loose and came across someone who acted like prey by running or screaming or both.

Probably most of the stories you hear about pits that make most of us think, "Oh, how awful those dogs must be," involve loose dogs of negligent owners and people who overreact. And maybe the other stories involve people or animals wandering onto the property of the pit bull. How many actual stories are left that involve crazed pit bulls running around and killing and/or maiming for no apparent reason? I'm starting to think that the answer is very, very few.

Other personal experiences have taught me that people can and will overreact around dogs. Back when I first moved into this house, my next-door neighbor related that the woman who lived here before me had a boyfriend who used to stay the night all the time. Apparently, the sheriff often came out to get the boyfriend because there was usually a warrant out for his arrest.

Well, one night, a police cruiser pulled into my driveway, and, when I went to answer the door, Casey slipped out into the sunroom with me. I was holding him by the collar while explaining to a skeptical officer that the people who had been here prior to my moving in were long gone.

"Actually, I've never even met them," I explained. "The house was a foreclosure. I have no idea where they are now."

The police officer was obviously not fond of dogs. He kept looking at Casey as though he were public enemy number one.

Casey wouldn't hurt anyone. If you force him to do something he doesn't want to do, he freezes up and turns into a 50-pound sack of dog fur. This lack of compliance was pointed out to me when he went to his four weeks of training at Top Dog Academy in Greenville. The husband/wife owners described him as passive/aggressive. Anytime they tried to teach him a new trick, he'd stare off at something in the distance and refuse to move. Or, he would roll over on his back and stay there whenever anyone attempted to get him to lie down.

Very recently I learned something about Casey's heritage. He has many of the same features as the breed known as a Plott hound. This type of dog was originally bred to hunt bears. I can't even begin to imagine Casey hunting a bear. He might bark at the bear. He might turn tail and run from a bear. He might stand there and shake so hard that the bear laughs itself to death. But, no, I can't picture Casey as a bear hunter.

Anyway, Casey let out a quiet "woof" and, as I tried to tell the officer that Casey would never bite, the police officer started reaching toward his Mace. To be frank, I was pissed off. This police officer came to my house without checking to see if the people he was looking for still even resided here. Then, when my dog barked—what most people generally know is a pretty typical response for dogs when strangers come to the door—the police officer responded with the possibility of Macing him? Really?! That happened over two years ago, and I still get tense when I think about it.

But now it also makes me question if a police officer responded that way to a thin, 50-pound lab/hound mix standing next to its owner and not snarling or growling, how often do law enforcement officials overreact when they come across pit bulls (or dogs they think are pit bulls) in the line of duty? One more reason it's probably a good idea to try to get the word out to people that pit bulls can be just as sweet as any other dog. (Months later, I will see an "Animal Precinct" special on Animal Planet about an undercover animal control officer. At one point, he talks about rescuing a pit bull from a dog fight in New York City. The dog gets placed and ends up living very happily with a family on Long Island. When the officer goes to visit it, he makes a remark that reminds me of my question. He says when he first saw the dog he knew it was just scared and that it would be okay once it calmed down, but added that the other police officers wanted to use a dart gun.)

Another related issue is how many attacks involve dogs that have been tethered on a chain or rope day in and day out. Depriving those dogs of companionship or exercise is inhumane and dangerous. Over thousands of years, canines have been domesticated as people bred the friendliest and most social ones. As a result, dogs crave the company of humans. They are also animals with a natural drive for physical activity. The Humane Society's Web site states that "an otherwise friendly and docile dog, when kept continuously chained, becomes neurotic, unhappy, anxious and often aggressive." Dogs have a flight-or-fight instinct. Chained dogs can't flee when they feel uncomfortable. If someone they perceive to be a threat approaches them (even a child), that person might become the target of an attack. Tethered or otherwise confined dogs can also get loose. Thus, many animal-related organizations encourage people to try to get anti-tethering laws passed in their communities.

My son is an adult and, except for Samantha, my dogs have never been around kids in my home. When they actually come across some out in public they understandably are a little freaked out by these tiny, noisy, impulsive little people. Imagine a dog tied up all the time with no socialization. How would it know how to react carefully and sensitively to a child? Even adults don't know how to do that sometimes based on what I've seen in the grocery store (including parents threatening to smack their own children or someone muttering under their breath what they'd do if that child throwing a tantrum were their own). Dogs need to learn what is acceptable behavior and what's not. They can't learn much from the tree or stake they're chained to. My dogs and cats co-exist well largely due to my constant reminders to the dogs to back off when the cats feel threatened. (Barney curled up next to the cats almost from the first night he spent on the couch, and later on groomed—by licking their heads and necks—the cats who would let him. Regardless, I spent a lot of time telling Barney not to chase the cats or reprimanding him when he tried too aggressively to engage them in play.)

Logic would indicate that the real issue is irresponsible dog owners—not an out-of-control type of dog. Yet, there's a definite theater of the absurd atmosphere that you will likely encounter when looking at news reports of pit bull attacks. As a former full-time journalist and a current freelance journalist, as well as a journalism instructor at a university, it makes me very sad and disappointed to see such a lack of responsible reporting.

For instance, I do a Google search about pit bull attacks and one of the first stories that comes up describes a boy who was attacked by a 92-pound pit bull that apparently just appeared out of the woods. The average weight of a pit bull is 35-55 pounds. There are some pit mixes that do reach as much as 110 pounds. But, anything over an 80-pounder would be one big pit. I try to picture Barney's projected adult frame with 92 pounds on it; he'd be so obese walking would likely tax his energy. Forget about stalking children from the woods, he'd have trouble stalking the food in his dog bowl.

Did the journalist look into this discrepancy? Question whether the pit was one hell of a fat dog for its breed? Look into whether the dog might not actually have been a pit or whether its size might be due to it being a combination of pit and some larger breed? No to all of the above. Or, at least the article didn't address any of this.

Another article on an "attack" right in the town in which I teach says, and, in the words of Dave Barry, *I'm not making this up*, that pit bulls broke the lock on their fence in order to get to another dog and injure it.

For a short period of time, Libby was getting out of the backyard until I realized she was doing it by pushing down on the latch on the gate. I put a piece of metal through the latch so she couldn't push it down anymore. Dogs get out of enclosures. They're masters at it. But breaking a lock? Did the pit bulls have crowbars? Or, perhaps it was a crappy lock? It's hard to know because the reporter doesn't offer any additional details.

By the way, I'll never forget walking through a middle class neighborhood in broad daylight with my son when he was about 12 and selling candy bars as a fundraiser for his sports team. There was one house with a metal fence around their backyard and two very big dogs jumping up and down, barking at us as if they wanted blood. With each jump, it seemed they managed to get a little closer to getting the top halves of their bodies almost over the top of the fence. And we weren't even on their side of the street. I don't remember what kind of dogs they were but I still remember that feeling of fear. If those aggressive animals had managed to finally get over that fence, we would have been in big trouble as there wasn't any way for us to get away from them if they chased us. The neighborhood was otherwise quiet. I had the feeling that a lot of people shut their shades and locked their doors or otherwise scampered out of sight when they saw us approaching with our $1-each candy bars for a worthy cause—seriously, it was frustrating, you'd think we were trying to unload swampland in Florida instead of keeping the local kids' football team afloat. Anyway, I have no idea how successful making fists and standing still would have been since there was more than one dog and both were revved up. To this day, I'm mad at the owners, not the dogs. They were courting disaster with a too-short fence and unsupervised, very territorial dogs. At the very least, anyone who has a dog that might be aggressive and could possibly get loose should not leave that dog outside when they're not home. Seems like the owner's failure to keep his or her dogs on their own property when dogs escape and attack is something that should be discussed in articles like the one mentioned above instead of reports that indicate it's all the fault of the dog(s).

Indeed, the Web site of the National Canine Research Council discusses case studies of incidents involving alleged pit bull attacks. The organization states that, "Newspaper and media accounts of dog attacks are often seriously flawed and/or incomplete," and lists a number of news stories and the apparent inaccurate information they contain. For example, they point out that at least four different news organizations reported that a woman had been killed by her pit bull; an autopsy later revealed she actually died of a drug overdose.

I surf over to the Humane Society of the United States Web site and look for information about dog bites. Fortunately, I find some comfort when pit bull does not instantly come up as the breed responsible for the most bites. The site states, "The breeds most commonly involved in both bite injuries and fatalities changes from year to year and from one area of the country to another, depending on the popularity of the breed."

Inasmuch as fatalities, statistics vary a bit depending on which source you look at, but on average, there are between 10 and 25 dog-bite-related fatalities in the United States each year. A commonly sited study is from the Journal of the American Medical Association. The study states that between 1979 and 1994 there were a total of 279 such human deaths. Deaths from dog attacks are extremely rare in other words.

Dog bites in general are not as rare. According to a survey from the National Centers for Disease Control and Prevention, almost 5 million people are bitten by dogs each year. There are about 74.8 million "owned" dogs in households in the U.S. according to the Humane Society of the United States. The population of the United States is over 300 million, so that's still an awful lot of people not bitten and a lot of dogs not biting. The number of those bitten who seek medical treatment drops to 800,000. Half of those bitten seriously enough to need treatment are children.

So what dogs bite? All are prone to biting in a given situation. According to the Web site of pit bull expert

Diane Jessup, "Often our perception is that only large, fierce, guardian type dogs bite, but this is simply not true. Labs, springier, [sic] cockers and sheepdogs are always near the top of lists detailing reported bites." With regard to dogs attacking children, Jessup notes, "Another way to put it in perspective is to realize that a child is *300 times more likely* to be killed by its parents or guardians than by a dog."

As noted at the Humane Society's site: "Although genetics do play some part in determining whether a dog will bite, other factors such as whether the animal is spayed or neutered, properly socialized, supervised, humanely trained, and safely confined play significantly greater roles. Responsible dog ownership of all breeds is the key to dog bite prevention."

The Humane Society's advice sounds reasonable. So, how did things get to be this way—with, for example, reports of pits breaking and entering like professional criminals without people even questioning it?

Based on the information I've seen so far, there's a mix out there of stories about pit bulls—or dogs identified as such—attacking other *animals*; stories about "pit bulls" biting *people*—sometimes badly, sometimes not; and very rare stories about dogs identified as bully breeds or pits *actually killing a human*. Taken all together, all these reports seem frightening and daunting, but, often, one or more of the below applies:

• a misidentification of breed,

• some human negligence involved (parents failing to adequately supervise children, dogs that have been chained and improperly socialized getting loose, owner drug and/or alcohol abuse, etc.).

Other factors that don't help the pit bull reputation include:

• a rise of popularity of pit bulls and mixes, leading to more dogs of this kind and more reports of bites from this type of dog,

• a rise in popularity in this dog amongst owners involved in criminal activities leading to an association between pit bulls and crime,

• the news media giving "top billing" to stories about pit bull-related incidents that might not even get coverage if it involved other dogs.

My guess is that some dog bites are misreported as well: i.e. Joe Sixpack gets bitten and has to go to the emergency room, but he feels silly reporting to the doctor that it was by his wife's _____ (fill in the blank with any innocent, cuddly-sounding dog), so he says it was a big, old, nasty pit or rottweiler.

What's more, our society loves perpetuating a good scary story. I grew up during the years Reagan was in office when everyone was scared silly about nuclear war. There were major budget theater releases such as "War Games," and made-for-tv movies on the topic. As if that weren't depressing enough, there were constant news reports, and discussions in schools and around the water coolers at businesses. For escapism from the cold war funfest that was the Reagan presidency, movies featured such relentlessly bloodthirsty characters as Freddy from the "Nightmare on Elm Street" series, Jason from "Friday the 13th" (parts 1 through who the heck knows how many?), and Michael Myers of the "Halloween" movies.

And how many urban legends are there floating around out there? We love to scare ourselves—facts can get in the way of that sometimes, so we ignore them.

When I talk to my students about the media shaping our world view, among other evidence, I point to an article about how the media widely reported on shark attacks during the summer of 2001. It seemed like one couldn't dip their toe in the ocean without it being bitten off by a shark.

And yet, the truth was shark attacks were actually down that summer. Worldwide there were only 72 unprovoked shark attacks (I don't know why anyone would provoke a shark attack—that joke always kills in class), according to a study done by the University of Florida. Statistically, chances of being attacked by a shark are extremely rare when you consider that the population of the world is almost 6.7 billion.

Pit bulls have co-existed with humans for far longer than their bad reputation has been perpetuated. Although the past few decades have led to a rise in fear of bully breeds, the history of these dogs is believed to go back to the time of the Romans who used the dogs in the "sport" of bull baiting.

Bull baiting was a form of entertainment (which might be a good example of why critics shouldn't complain quite so much about the advent of television) and worship of the warrior god. It involved tying a bull to a post so that it could only move about 30 feet. The object was for dogs to immobilize the bull. In a variation, success involved a dog clamping onto the bull's snout. Selective breeding of the best fighting dogs led to what may have been the ancestors of modern-day pit bulls.

This activity continued and was popular in Great Britain until it was banned in 1835. For the bloodthirsty in need of an alternative way to spend their free time, ratting was developed. Rats were placed in a *pit* (hence, the name *pit bull*) with a dog. The larger number of rats killed, the better the dog did in the "contest." It's commonly believed that terriers (for agility) were mixed with bull-baiting dogs to get successful pit fighters. I guess there wasn't enough grotesque excitement in these events because someone got the bright idea of fighting dogs against each other.

A number of sources note that, as pit bulls were bred, they were selected for animal aggression—not human aggression. As "Pit Bulls for Dummies" puts it, "In the heat of battle, the dogs must discriminate between biting another dog and biting a human" because referees and handlers were often in the rings during the fights. A human aggressive pit bull would likely make a horrible fighter and also wouldn't be bred. Thus, even though dog fighting is vile, those breeding dogs weren't necessarily perpetuating a *human aggressive* dog.

Because of its reputation for strength and courage, in the early 1900s, the American Pit Bull Terrier became a popular dog in our country. Posters during World War I featured this type of dog as an American mascot. Among other American icons, movie star Fred Astaire was a pit bull owner.

Those responsible and caring humans who own pits today seem as infatuated as I've become. Even as I ask around and look through chat rooms on the Internet, I hear and read account after account of basically the same scenario: Someone comes across a pit bull in need of a home. Reluctantly, they take a chance on the dog and end up amazed by how loyal and sweet it turns out to be.

Overall, there appears to be four categories into which people fall when it comes to pits. The first group is those who love the dogs and are educated about the pit breeds.

The second group is the one that gives pits the benefits of the doubt on the assumption that: *It's not the dog that's the problem, it's the owner. Treat a dog well and you have a kind and well behaved dog. Treat the dog badly and you might end up with a vicious animal.* This is the group that I used to belong to, and it's a reasonable stance, except that I'm finding out that there are some super sweet dogs with crappy owners, and some not-always-so-lovable dogs with great owners.

The third group is not sure what to think. They've heard evidence for both sides and haven't made up their minds either way.

Those in the fourth group are positive that pit bulls are the hounds of the devil, and people in that group always seem to know of a not just one but a number of people whose (to paraphrase Jimmy Fallon) faces have been chewed off by pit bulls.

I have absolutely ended up in the first group. As I type this, I look down at Barney who is conked out at my feet. I can say few things with absolutely certainty, but I'm positive this dog will never, ever intentionally harm me.

Even if I didn't have that gut feeling, I could also take solace in some statistics. Journalist John Stossel does a good job of questioning common beliefs. His book "Give Me a Break," includes a "death list" that shows causes of death in America and yearly averages. Plastic bags claim 25 people per year and drowning in toilets claims 6, according to the list. So, if the statistic about pit bulls causing 3 human deaths per year is correct, I'm safer with Barney than a plastic bag and have less reason to fear him than my bathroom.

But, the other groups had to come from somewhere, even though, for a while, pits enjoyed widespread popularity. When did things go wrong for the pit reputation-wise? There isn't a clear answer. Some blame— and not unfairly—those who fight dogs. For one, un-neutered male dogs tend to be more aggressive than neutered males. Dog fighters don't neuter dogs for a number of reasons, including the desire to breed the best fighters to get even better future fighters.

According to "Pit Bulls for Dummies," a group lobbied against dogfights, which was already illegal, in the 1970s. This caused a "crackdown" on dog fighting by law enforcement, which brought negative publicity to pit bulls themselves and pushed dog fighting underground. Ironically, the move underground may have resulted in extremely inhumane treatment of the dogs by the dog fighters (for example, dogs beaten with clubs to increase aggression toward canine opponents).

Breeding of pit bulls for those who want to own one to appear macho leads to further problems. Puppies need to be with their brothers and sisters for a certain period of time. If a puppy is removed from the litter too early, the dog can become too aggressive. The reason is that dogs socialize each other, learning not to bite too hard during play and so forth. Those people who don't understand or don't care and separate puppies from their siblings prematurely are helping to possibly send more aggressive pits out into the world. When a breed gets popular, more and more shoddy breeders pop up who set up backyard or basement pens leading to more problems with improperly socialized dogs.

By the way, pits are extremely cute as puppies. Seeing them makes it very hard to believe anyone could ever peg such a dog as a future fighter or killer. Amanda once emailed me a picture of one of her pit bulls when it was a puppy. I printed it out and it hung on my office wall. Many students "oohed" and "aahed" at the photo, followed by expressing surprise when informed that they were looking at a pit bull. One day recently a couple brought two 6-week-old puppies to the dog park. One was white, and the other brown and white. It was neat to see what Barney has developed from. For their size (about 8 or 9 inches in height), their feet were overly large with a comical roundness to them. Their tails never stopped wagging in the air as they explored everything they possibly could around them. One stopped to sniff a tennis ball that was way too big to fit in the pup's mouth. The couple in their 20s had brought the puppies and, while the woman seemed very maternal in her treatment of them, the man kept engaging the puppies in play that made them growl aggressively. It was a funny growl, the kind of threatening noise one might take as seriously as a toddler with a plastic bat. But it was hard to believe this guy was doing any favors to the dog or humans by encouraging behavior that one day might change from unbelievably adorable to very scary.

Another problem is lack of education. As already mentioned, misidentification of other dogs as pit bulls means these dogs might get the blame for attacks or bites more often than they should.

Also, I've been reading about dogs for a number of years, but never realized there's a difference between dogs with "dog aggression" and dogs with "human aggression." These terms keep coming up now as I do research on pit bulls. If a dog is *dog* or *animal* aggressive it doesn't mean that it will be aggressive to *people*. Pit experts believe that people who don't know the difference, which is a large portion of the public apparently, erroneously fear that a dog who attacks a cat or other animal will suddenly become thirsty for human blood and start attacking people. Shelters all over the country are filled with surrendered pit bulls and such mistaken beliefs are a part of the reason for surrenders.

Those who are in the know dispute the myth that pits are likely to be aggressive to humans. The United Kennel Club even recommends against using American Pit Bull Terriers as guard dogs because "they are extremely friendly, even with strangers." They add that, "Aggressive behavior toward humans is uncharacteristic of the breed."

The American Temperament Test Society (www.ATTS.org) is a not-for-profit organization established to promote "uniform temperament evaluation of purebred and spayed/neutered mixed-breed dogs." ATTS tests various dog breeds for temperament, which is basically the way a dog behaves in an environment, given its mental abilities and physical characteristics taken as a whole. The tests involve measuring dogs for stability, shyness, aggressiveness and friendliness. The American Pit

Bull Terriers tested at 84.3 percent. The American Staffordshire Terrier tested at 83.4 percent. The Staffordshire Bull Terrier tested at 88.8 percent. Thus, they compare respectably to popular family pet breeds, such as the Labrador retriever (91.8 percent) and the Irish setter (90 percent). Incidentally, a miniature bull terrier (a breed sharing some characteristics with the pit breeds) scored at 100 percent.

Midwest Rescue of Illinois, Inc. suggests that pit bulls are used as fighting dogs because they will do anything to please their human owners, even fight to the death. In other words, they're singled out for punishment *because of* their loyalty.

Besides alleged human aggression, another belief that doesn't help things is that pit bulls have locking jaws. This locking jaw myth probably comes at least in part from the whole bull baiting era. The story goes that pits have jaws that are so strong it makes it impossible to get them off of anything or anyone they have bitten. In truth, studies show that their jaw mechanisms and structure is no different from any other breed. They might, however, be a little more tenacious or bullheaded than other dogs; when they get a hold of something, they are determined not to let go.

At work, I start asking around about people's knowledge of pit bulls. One of my students, who used to work as an animal control officer in Texas, tells me his experiences with pits didn't reflect all the hysteria that surrounds the dogs. He says that he would prefer being chased by a pit bull, as opposed to some breeds, because pits tend to tire more easily, and, if you can jump a fence to escape from them, there's not much they can do about it. On the other hand, not much will stop a German shepherd because they are very athletic and smart dogs that aren't easily deterred.

Most of what I'm learning is a relief, especially because I'm now in love with Barney. I probably drive him crazy. I can't stop staring at, kissing or making cooing noises to him, especially when he looks up at me in apparent deep thought, causing little *wrinklies* on his forehead. He's such a handsome little guy now that I'm getting used to his features. And I also admire his resiliency. One would think he never had a care in his life. The recovery power of dogs (and cats) that I've seen over and over never fails to amaze me.

Sadly, as Barney continues to get better, Libby is doing worse. I take her to the dog park on a Sunday afternoon along with Penny, my Corgi mix. It's a beautiful, sunny day; the park is crowded with people and dogs. Too many to count. It's so crowded that it takes forever just to get into the first fenced-in area, which leads to the gates to both the area for big dogs and the adjacent one for smaller dogs.

There's a black Lab on the other side of the gate sniffing at the new arrivals, including Libby, and Libby is straining at the leash. I let her off and open the gate. Instead of running for the center of the park in search of dogs to romp with as she usually does, she growls and jumps on top of the black Lab. There's a lot of commotion as I try to get inside the gate. Other people leaving are blocking my way. "Whose dogs are these?" I hear someone shout. Meanwhile, Libby is still on top of the Lab and the Lab is yelping. Someone pulls Libby off and the Lab's person comes and smothers it with affection.

I'm finally able to get to Libby. Everyone is looking at us as though we're terrorists and I can't blame them. That was a bad scene! Libby is really starting to scare me. This is the first time she's ever jumped on a dog like that at the dog park. She's done it at home, but it's usually been because of jealousy over or a toy, during times when our daily routines get out of whack (which stresses her out), or for some other "reason." This is totally random as far as I can tell.

Only minutes later, she's running around the park, playing peacefully like nothing ever happened. I've read about dogs who have extreme behavior changes due to neurological problems and I'm wondering if Libby might have something similar going on. I sure hope not. The dogs I read about only became increasingly worse, and I remember pitying them and their people for the ensuing struggles and pain they endured because of the unpredictable behavior.

I take a deep breath and head for the park bench trying to act as nonchalant as Libby. I hope this was only a fluke. But I have the feeling it wasn't.

Chapter 5

Libby remains under close watch for the next few weeks. I no longer bring her to the park, which makes me sad because she loved it and it was a great way for her to burn off a lot of her energy. But, I can't take the chance that she might jump on another dog.

I have good reason to be worried. I didn't see it happen, but I'm pretty sure she bit Samantha, my oldest dog. Samantha is in great shape and most people are surprised to learn she'll be 10 years old this year. Now, though, she has about a 2-inch wound on the left side of her face under her eye. Libby probably went after Samantha in a food-guarding incident. (Barney, who still continues to play with Libby and sometimes pushes her too far, gets a very similar looking but smaller mark on his neck a couple days later.) Plus, it suddenly became impossible to get Sammy to eat unless I put her food in a bowl, bring her into the bedroom, close the door and pet her as she chews.

Libby has stepped up her food aggression since Barney came in. I'm pretty sure there's a connection there. Libby has never felt too secure as far as I can tell, and having yet another dog around isn't helping. Another reason I stopped taking in animals a couple years ago was because it felt like we were at a tipping point. The size of the house and space available to the animals, as well as my household budget and busy work schedule, all seemed stretched and it didn't seem fair to them to bring in any new furry creatures. In addition, I read a convincing argument that serving as a foster for animals allows you to help a greater number of animals over a period of time than you can when you adopt. At some point in the distant future, I plan to have maybe only a few cats and a dog or two while fostering others.

I really, really hate that Samantha is hurt. Her only other injury in her entire life was when her tail got caught in the screen door when she was coming in the house. That was years ago and, to this day, she still will not come through an open door unless it is all the way open. Even then she will push at it with her nose first as a precaution.

I'm trying very hard to forgive Libby and to look for ways to help her hopefully become less aggressive. I consider buying a muzzle, as one Web site recommends, but then read in "Bandit" that muzzles can restrict the airflow to dogs, who breathe primarily through their noses, and can cause them to panic. As an asthma sufferer since the age of 16, I am very sympathetic to how frightening constricted breathing can be.

There is now another big "tub" of food next to the first one in the kitchen, which will hopefully signal there's plenty to go around and that Libby doesn't need to guard it. (I don't switch to individual bowls of food and scheduled feeding times for each dog. It's possible if I did so and stood guard while everyone ate, I could correct individual incidents of food aggression. However, I've been free feeding my dogs for about five years and it has always worked up until now. Plus, I'm not that organized and my schedule is hectic. I really need free feeding to continue to work.)

Meanwhile, almost three months after he first showed up at my house, Barney continues to have stomach problems. Our third and most recent trip to the veterinarian was upsetting. She told me she wasn't sure what was wrong with Barney, but that he might have irritable bowel syndrome. If so, it'll be something that might affect him his entire life. It's also apparently hard to diagnose. Surgery would be involved to get a stomach sample for a diagnosis. I'm not ready to subject Barney to surgery that wouldn't even cure him or make him feel better. And it might not even be IBS.

Barney is doing well enough to get his shots, and he's now up to 37 pounds—so, when the vet tells me to come back with Barney in three weeks for a checkup—I decide to try switching Barney's diet to exclusively a type of dry kibble for dogs with sensitive stomachs. It costs more than double what I usually pay for a bag of dog food, but results can be seen in days. Now, 90 percent of the time, he's okay. I have never been so happy to see regular feces in my entire life. The other 10 involves diarrhea. And, believe me, that beats 50/50 or worse prior percentages.

Since this diet is working, maybe he just needs a little more time for his stomach to heal. He's eating well, gaining weight and drinking plenty of fluids. Also, in addition to eating his own feces (which I know isn't pleasant but is still relevant to the discussion of the course of "treatment"), Barney had been getting into the cats' litter boxes, so I move those where he can't get to them, and that also helps as far as I can tell.

While all this is taking place, I find out about a kit the Humane Society makes available to help get anti-tethering laws passed. If Barney had been inside with a family who took care of him, he wouldn't have to endure these ongoing stomach troubles. It makes me think about the hunting dogs next door and other dogs that are kept outside without the regular access to meals that they might have if they were inside with their owners. If asked, my neighbors would probably say that they regularly feed their dogs, but there have been times when those dogs have been skin and bones, and God knows what they ended up eating to keep themselves going all those hours out there alone.

I go to the Care2: The Petition Site (www.thepetitionsite.com) and create a petition asking people to sign as a show of support that tethering should be banned in Pitt County. I begin hoping to reach Pitt County residents. My friend, Joy, who started her own nonprofit to help cats and who has tons of email addresses of animal lovers, sends it out. In a matter of days, the petition is spreading via email across the country and beyond. In only four days, over 200 people sign. I get some great responses along with the signatures, including:

•"It is unfortunate that Pitt County is one of the few counties that still allows…tethering of dogs. There are SO many reasons that a dog should not be tethered I cannot even begin to address them all. Dogs should be a part of the family, not some forgotten possession at the end of a chain in the back yard."—Tina Williams, North Carolina

•"Dogs are pack animals. They need the companionship of other beings. To tie them up for their entire lives is inhumane and cruel. They are exposed to all sorts of weather...what a tortured, lonely life! Why have a dog (or any other animal) if you aren't going to treat it with love, kindness and respect!!?"—Laura Horning, Ohio

•"Dogs are a man's best friend so I thought, obviously not in Pitt County. Maybe it is time for change; it is after all the 21st century. Lets chain a few humans up and see how they like it!" *[sic]* —Ann Boyce, United Kingdom.

I also write a letter to the editor about the issue and it's published in the Greenville newspaper. I follow up with a letter to the state representative from my district. And wait…

In the meantime, Barney doesn't let his stomach troubles get him down—or at least not keep him from settling in and its accompanying behavior. He has turned into a chewing machine. When he sits next to me on the couch, he likes to chew on my hands. I take this as a good sign because he's doing it in a playful way and knows that it's not appropriate to bite down too hard. Some of my other dogs did this in the past early on after being adopted. Inasmuch as a pit bull's jaw being stronger than that of other dogs, I personally can't tell any difference in strength. Yes, I know if he wanted to hurt me, he could. That he can but doesn't, is a beautiful thing. Dogs constantly hold back so much of their force to please humans and it's another reason they're such remarkable companions.

Barney is also teething. Surprisingly, he doesn't like to play tug of war with a rope with me (he prefers when I throw a toy so he can retrieve it). He has been chewing like crazy on all the furniture though. Over a period of weeks, he has gnawed the paint off of the entire front edge of my coffee table, and the computer desk in the kitchen has what looks like a giant bite mark out of the side from Barney chomping off bits and pieces.

None of this is particularly upsetting to me. If it's a choice between a brand new living room set and no pets, or a bunch of secondhand pieces and the companionship, I choose the latter.

I guess I have a laissez-faire attitude about training my pets, but don't think that's such a bad thing for my lifestyle. I mean, I don't throw dinner parties where I expect Duke or Lady to sit quietly in the corner the entire evening with absolutely no interest in any of the table scraps that fall on the floor. I've seen people who believe their dogs have to be as well trained and well behaved as Lassie. I admit I'm a bit jealous that their dogs don't jump up on random party guests in a living room full of strangers or that they actually sit on command in a crowded park even with a game of Frisbee going on mere feet away. Getting my dogs to act like that isn't a priority though.

As mentioned before, there's the school of thought that: Treat a dog well, you have a good dog; bad dogs come from unfit owners. The problem with that theory is that there are plenty of exceptions. Even Samantha, my black Lab whom I have had since she was a puppy, has her questionable moments. She doesn't like strangers to pet her when she's on a leash, especially men. I took her up to work with me one night when I had some stuff to do in the office and she growled at the janitor in the hallway. I had a good hold of her leash, but she made the janitor so nervous he wouldn't pass her—he actually went out the front doors and around the outside of the building to get to where he was going.

She also makes some of the veterinarians who have given her shots nervous because of how stiff her body becomes and how deep between her legs her tail gets. She's never bitten anyone, but her body language screams "warning!" Off leash at the dog park, she's fine with people and other dogs. I guess she feels uncomfortable and more vulnerable when she's on a leash.

The only reasons I can think of for her behavior are: It's in her nature to be suspicious of strangers, i.e. just another personality trait, like her love of the water. Or, it might also be that, even though she was nuts about him at the time, my ex-boyfriend played too rough with her. During the first year after we adopted her, it was always the same. He would roll around on the floor and they would "wrestle" and, at first, it would be all fun and games. Then, he would keep playing and she'd give a warning growl that things were getting more intense. My ex would ignore it and after a few more minutes would let out this loud "owww" and stand up with a small, bloody mark, usually on his forehead. He'd be all offended that she nipped at him and the game would be over. At least for the moment. The next day it would start all over again.

From my experience, it's usually guys who engage dogs in rough play. And, not surprisingly, the statistics show that men are more likely than women to be bitten by dogs.

When I asked one of my classes of about 18 students if anyone had ever been bitten by a pit bull, only one student—a male—responded. I talked to him after class for a few minutes and he told me that it was his girlfriend's dog that he had known for about two years and that he had been playing too rough with it until it ended up biting him and drawing blood.

Anyway, my ex also was big on training and he read that when puppies whine, you should fill a jar with pennies and shake it at them till they stop. Back then, I was much less educated about dogs and more likely to take for granted that, if it was published in a book, it must be true. So, although I wanted no part of the actual jar shaking, I didn't object when he did it each time Samantha started making noise. And it worked. Soon, she merely had to see the jar and she would stop. But I think now of how it must have been frightening to her as a small puppy to be in a dark room (she slept nights in a crate in the bedroom and her bedtime was earlier than ours) and have some tall, shadowy figure come in and make a lot of loud, scary noise whenever she cried.

I know that good, positive training can have brilliant effects that benefit the dog and owner. Training that teaches a dog not to run out into the street, for instance. I also have a consistent fear that my animals won't find good homes if anything happens to me. It's likely that the better trained they are, the better the chances of them being adopted. But, thanks to the ex, I've also learned that some training can solve one problem while creating another.

And, unfortunately, no matter how well trained a dog, sometimes human ignorance can still override it. This is illustrated one sunny Sunday when I'm at the dog park with Maggy. It's not particularly crowded because it's about 6 p.m. There are maybe 10 people and their dogs in the "large dog" part of the park. There's a couple with a puppy in the "small dog area." Suddenly, the woman from that couple starts asking if anyone knows whose dog is outside the fence. A number of people go over to look. I watch from where I'm sitting—about 30 feet away. The dog is medium-sized with brown fur. There's speculation as to where it came from. I hear the woman say it's a pit bull and that it looks like it's trying to "get at" some of the dogs in the park. Someone else more reasonable says that it must not be a stray because it looks pretty well fed. In the midst of all the commotion, the dog's owner strolls up and nonchalantly lets the dog in through the park gate as he follows behind.

People go back to what they were doing, but the incident bothers me for a couple of reasons. First, now that I see him up close, the canine doesn't look remotely pit bull-like. Second, the woman who brought the dog to everyone's attention had made such a big deal out of the dog's mere presence one would have thought it was a dingo carrying a human baby in its jaw.

The dog's owner is at fault too, though. Like any college town, Greenville is not without its share of citizens driving too fast, so it was not a good idea to let a dog run around without a leash. On the other hand, I guess they were walking over from a nearby apartment complex (of which there are at least three), and it's pretty impressive that this dog knew to come right to the park, even with his owner trailing far behind him. Regardless, it is so indicative of the panic that surrounds dogs, and it's easy to see how people's overreactions can lead to hysteria that in turn leads to sensationalized news reports and canines being destroyed for no good reason. In this case, the woman who started it all was a dog owner. She should have known better. I guess since her dog is a puppy, maybe she is just starting to learn about dogs.

Unfortunately, as I'm still finding out, it is especially easy to be ignorant when it comes to pit bulls. Like I mentioned before, pits are typically classified as three breeds: the American Pit Bull Terrier, the American Staffordshire Terrier, and the Staffordshire Bull Terrier. But, the issue is more complicated because a bunch of other breeds have similar characteristics. And, not everyone seems to agree on which dogs fall under the pit bull umbrella. It's a bigger umbrella for some groups. For instance, Midwest Rescue of Illinois, Inc. describes pits as being the above three breeds "and others."

The ASPCA's Web site relates, "There is a great deal of confusion and fear associated with the term 'pit bull.' This is a label commonly used for a type of short-coated large terrier, anywhere from 40–80 pounds, characterized by a wide skull, powerful jaws, and a muscular, stocky body." However, somewhat confusingly, the ASPCA states that the Staffordshire Bull Terrier "shares a similar body type" to pit bulls, but are "substantially smaller dogs." (The Staffordshire Bull Terrier's weight range is 24-38 pounds.)

Wikipedia states that "several physically similar breeds...are often termed 'pit bull' in English speaking countries, including the American Pit Bull Terrier, American Staffordshire Terrier, Staffordshire Bull Terrier, Perro de Presa Canario, Cane Corso, Dogo Argentino, Alano Espanol, Japanese Tosa, and Dogue de Bordeaux, among others.

Kind of makes my head hurt trying to get it all straight, but one thing I do know for sure after today's dog park incident is that the average person might identify any dog with any sort of similar characteristic to an actual pit as a pit bull. In the case of the woman in the park, the resemblance between the dog she labeled a "pit bull" and anything in that actual category was that both have four legs and a tail.

Not everything I witness is irritating. Some things I see are actually heartening, even somewhat funny. For instance, about a mile up the road from where I live is a trailer. I've seen a black and white pit running loose around the trailer a number of times (not the funny part). I started seeing this dog not long after Barney showed up at my house, and briefly wondered if there was a connection, since this was the only other pit I've noticed in my area. But, I don't think there is. For one, this dog looks like a purebred, not a mix like Barney. And it is located a mile from my house, which doesn't seem long when driving on this long country road, but, which I'm sure would be a trek for a 6-month-old puppy.

Anyway, as I pass the trailer one day on my way to work, I see a telephone repair van parked on the opposite side of the street. Next to it is a repairman who is unable to work because he's being interrupted by the black and white pit. The canine is on his hind legs smothering the man with love, and I can see from the man's face that he is not only not terrified, he's slouching, appearing resigned to letting this dog get it out of his system so that work can resume.

Incidentally, around here, the opposite of keeping dogs tied up or penned 24 hours a day is letting one's dog(s) run loose. I guess this worked well years ago. When I was growing up on Long Island, there was a German shepherd named Mush who lived in a house on the corner of our block in suburban neighborhood. None of the kids on the block was afraid of Mush because they knew the only thing he didn't like in life was cars. Every time a car would come down the street, Mush would chase it. I can still picture him barking at the back tires of a station wagon from what seemed like inches away as it drove up the block. No one ever questioned it. Mush basically did this for years until he was too old. None of the drivers ever stopped—at least as far as I know.

Nowadays, it wouldn't be long before someone did stop, tracked down Mush's owner and threatened to sue. Plus, there are many more cars these days and many of them are going too fast to be able to slow down if a loose dog ran in front of them. So, although it's nice to see that not all dogs out here in the country are spending their entire lives confined, the loose roaming doesn't seem to be much of an alternative.

In the midst of all my experiences, Barney keeps on doing what puppies do so well—he's growing like crazy. When he came into the house that first night, he was the same exact height as my Corgi mix. He is now at least half a foot taller than her from paws to back.

Probably a combination of his stage in development and his continued recovery have also led Barney to become, well…kind of a pain in the ass lately. Sitting down on the couch with a snack is out because—no matter how many times I tell him "no" and gently push him down—he'll pop right back up again and try to get the food.

He's stubborn as heck. Kind of like a bulldozer with fur. His arms (or, front legs, depending on how anthropomorphic you are) are getting thicker, reminding me of a chubby toddler. Except he's all muscle and not one ounce of fat, so it actually starts to hurt my wrists after I've pushed him down repeatedly.

He'll also try to engage the other dogs in play, and, when they refuse, he'll back up a few steps, wag his tail and bark repeatedly. Saying, "Barney stop," does not work, even when I raise my voice. The only thing that gets his attention during one of these barking fits is to spray a bit of water on him from a spray bottle.

While he does pretty well on a leash, the only exercise he can get off leash is in my medium-sized backyard. And, as he grows, it definitely isn't enough room. I start taking him on walks around the backyard area that isn't fenced in and which is much larger. I've stopped worrying that my neighbors might try to re-claim him. He looks so much better and bigger than before that, if he ever did belong to them, I doubt they'd even believe it was the same dog. Besides, I'd just whip out the vet bills and that would likely nip any claims in the bud.

Then it rains for days on end and the property is full of huge, muddy puddles. Over a weekend, we're all rained in and Barney is full of energy. He's driving me crazy. He won't stop jumping all over Libby, which is normally a good thing because when the two of them play together (which involves a lot of short chases, tug of war and basic doggie wrestling) they tire each other out. Libby can't play right now though because one of her nails has broken off, leaving a bleeding, uncovered nail pad. I'm running out of rooms to keep them all separated, but have to take the chance of letting Libby back in the bedroom with Samantha (whose face is healing nicely). We are absolutely at full capacity. I'm out of patience, losing my temper and shouting a whole lot more than I typically do.

Most of the time, I never yell at the dogs or cats. I know this is a bad patch that will pass. There are definite highs and lows to living with multiple animals. Plus, there's a conflict going on at work that's eating at me. I grin my teeth and bear it, knowing this too shall pass.

Around mid-April the lawn needs to be mowed for the first time this year. The sun is shining and it's a warm but comfortable temperature outside. I'm mowing the fenced-in part of the backyard and all the dogs except Casey are outside with me. The sight hound/Lab mix can jump fences, even the 6-foot one in my backyard, so he can only come outside on a leash.

Out of the corner of my eye, I see Barney pick something up and then flip it. He looks totally taken by surprise and a little scared, so I rush over to investigate. The object that he flipped turns out to be a small snapping turtle. I had no idea that snapping turtles could live on land and am clueless about how it got inside the fence. I always thought they pretty much kept to the bottom of lakes. I also have had a longtime fear of snapping turtles. The thought of them reaching the size of a small boulder and lurking underwater waiting for some hapless creature to swim by and then using their extremely strong jaws to grab hold of their prey…well, it gives me the shivers.

This snapping turtle is maybe four inches long from nose to back side of shell and its tail adds about two more inches to its overall length. Its face is much more pointy than that of a box turtle. And it's covered in dirt, possibly for camouflage, like a miniature Rambo. It's actually kind of cute.

There are still a number of rain-filled holes the dogs have dug in the backyard. I guess these holes are attractive to snapping turtles, even in a backyard frequented by dogs. It would help if I had some gloves that would let me pick it up. I should be more prepared for stuff like this. I knew there would be various wild animals around here when I moved in, but mostly envisioned the cute, furry ones.

I can't move too far from the turtle because it's all I can do to get the dogs to stay back, so going inside in search of protective hand gear is not an option. The shovel is nearby. After a number of very gentle (not to mention terrified and extremely quick) shoves to its rear, the snapping turtle crawls onto the shovel. At this point, I'm starting to wonder if maybe it isn't a snapping turtle. It's so calm and I didn't actually see it snap at Barney. That's when it opens up its pointy mouth and hisses at me.

Well, that clears up any doubts.

Holding the shovel by the handle, I carefully move into the garage. I close the door to the yard and then open the garage door and put shovel, hissing turtle and all on the ground outside. I close the door. A few minutes later, a check reveals that the turtle is long gone.

Yet even an hour later, the image of Barney's surprised face as he flipped the turtle keeps coming into my mind. It's that kind of look that makes me feel all maternal and reminds me of how, when my son was little, there were always those playground scrapes or bee stings that I couldn't protect him from, no matter how much I wanted to.

It also turns out to be another indicator of Barney's good nature. He didn't growl or show any other signs of aggression in spite of being taken by surprise. There's probably something ironic or poetic about a pit bull being bit by a snapping turtle, and maybe a better writer than I could really elaborate on that irony and so forth. Personally, the best I can come up with at the moment is that it's weird.

Later on, I do some Web surfing and find out that the snapping turtle is the pit bull of the turtle world.

According to the Western North Carolina Nature Center's Web site: "The Snapping Turtle has a bad reputation with the public due to its supposedly aggressive nature and because it is believed by many to heavily prey on game fishes and young ducks. In reality, the snapping turtle is largely a scavenger, prowling the pond and river bottom searching for diseased or dying fish and other small animals...An occasional baby duck or other waterfowl may be eaten but many more are probably eaten by feral dogs, cats, and other wild animals...with the Snapper then being unjustly accused. The snapping turtle has long been eaten and relished by man and is used primarily in soups and stews."

The parallels are uncanny. Here's yet another animal with a misunderstood power and, much like humans abusing pit bulls in dog fights, snapping turtles are probably in more danger from humankind than the other way around.

And just totally FYI (which is what I always say to my students when I'm adding some slightly related bit of trivia into my lecture), another site notes that when these turtles are encountered in the water, they are "passive" and usually retreat from threat. On land, they might lunge at potential enemies. When they're on land, it tends to be in the spring when males are moving from pond to pond and females are searching for nesting sites. In other words, they're wandering around looking for love. Adult snapping turtles can range from 10 to 50 pounds in the wild. This makes me extremely grateful that the one in my backyard was definitely not even a pound. If it were 10 pounds or over, well…I think then I would just have had to completely relinquish my backyard and move to a new house. There's a limit to enlightenment I guess.

Earlier on the same day of the pit bull/snapping turtle showdown, I had received an email from my state representative recommending contacting my county commissioners to try to get the anti-tethering ordinance passed in Pitt County. Originally, that's where I thought I should start, but two people recommended contacting my state rep. That misstep cost me a month. I prepare another package of information and a letter, and send it to one of my representing commissioners. While mowing the un-fenced part of my yard on my ride-on lawnmower, I repeatedly pass the tethered dog next door. He's surrounded by holes that I guess he dug out of sheer boredom and need of exercise. I wish that a month hadn't just been wasted.

A week or so later, I'm reading Ken Foster's new book, "The Dogs I Have Met," in which he talks about taking his dog to a new dog park. After a number of visits to one dog park, his dog started to get territorial and so he had to switch to a different one (park, not dog). It's like a revelation to me. I remember Libby on her best behavior on our first couple of trips to the park. After numerous visits, I'll bet she was getting territorial and that's why she jumped on that dog that was already inside the gate. It's such a simple idea, I can't believe I didn't think of it before. The more I read about and think I know about dogs, the more I realize that there is always so much more to learn about what makes these animals tick.

That same week, as I'm about to leave for work and letting Barney in from the backyard (his housetraining is coming along nicely), he jumps up and puts his paws on my stomach in greeting (which he tends to do even if it's after being outside for less than 10 minutes). I look at how round his face has become and finally realize what it is about his features that I've been trying to figure out. Because his face is flatter and more round than my other dogs' faces, it gives him a more human appearance. The others do very human-like things from time to time, but Barney actually reminds me of a human child.

About three days later, it's around midnight on Saturday when something far less touching happens. I'm up watching tv and let the dogs out into the backyard. They're out for about five minutes when I hear yelps and barks signaling a significant scuffle. I run out into the backyard in bare feet, something I would never do in a non emergency.

In the corner of the yard, Libby is on top of one of the other dogs. At first, I think it's Barney but it turns out to be Penny, my sweet Corgi mix. I pick up the water dish and carry it with me to throw it between them. By the time I get to them, the other dogs have already broken up the fight.

Penny comes inside with me. I leave Libby outside. Penny's ears, which usually point straight up, are down. Her head and neck are covered with mud and saliva. She has a bit of blood in her ear and is missing a small patch of fur on the top of her head. I feel sick. Penny is the last dog I would ever think would provoke Libby. It sounded a lot worse than it turned out to be, but this is no longer a bunch of random occurrences I can write off. This is a pattern.

As I'm calming Penny down, I see headlights in my driveway and I put on a robe before answering the knock at the door. A sheriff, who, as it turns out, lives two houses down from me, is standing on my doorstep.

"I heard a lot of noise and it sounded like maybe one of your dogs was being attacked by a wild animal," he says. "I wanted to make sure they were okay."

I've never met him before, and he's in full uniform, so I'm wondering if he is just about to go on shift or maybe just coming home. Either way, I'm touched by his concern and amazed at how quickly he responded. It's also embarrassing though, and I hope he doesn't get the impression that my animals aren't properly supervised.

Oh, Libby. Libby, Libby, Libby, I think when I'm back inside. She's a beautiful, healthy dog. Her whole body is a long, slinky, muscular frame. During many of our initial uneventful trips to the dog park, I noticed how many guys loved her. Most of the men she ran up to couldn't resist petting her, and I remember thinking she'd probably make a great pet for a single male. She's in the prime of her life. Actually putting her down would be horrific. And, in spite of her issues with other dogs, this is still a dog I curl up next to at night.

Maybe I can get my friend, Joy, to help me find her a new home. She'd have to go somewhere with no other dogs, and definitely no kids to be on the safe side. I talked myself out of taking her to the vet after the park incident, but I know my first call on Monday morning will be to see if there's a medical solution.

At the vet two days later, I sit in the waiting room. Libby makes a huge show of tugging on her leash and wanting to jump up and put her paws on everything, including the reception counter. There's an elderly woman sitting in the corner with her dog—a pit bull! I don't get time to talk with her though because she's quickly called in. The dog looks strong enough to pull the woman like a horse pulling a car, but patiently walks next to her as the woman shuffles behind her walker.

Although the attack on Penny made this appointment seem urgent, over the past couple of days, I've been wondering whether a vet can do anything to help. I almost cancelled the appointment three or four times since I made it; I'm wondering whether I should have gone straight to a trainer. My answer comes in a few minutes when I'm called into one of the examination rooms. A veterinary assistant enters with five photocopied pages on dog aggression from a book. She hands them to me and explains that I need to get Libby to see me as dominant. She recommends teaching her simple commands, such as "sit" and "come." The problem is that Libby knows these commands—well, she knows "come" anyway—she just doesn't necessarily obey. I wonder if there's a "Please, don't attack randomly" or "Get the heck off that poor, innocent dog" command.

The assistant tells me that Libby will feel more reassured if she knows I'm the one in control—that will make her more confident and less likely to bite other dogs. I would have thought maybe Libby noticed I was the more dominant one of the two of us when I was driving her to the dog park or lugging home large bags of food. But, okay, I'll give it a try. She recommends giving it about two to three weeks and, if I still have a problem, coming back and discussing the possibility of anti-anxiety medication (for Libby, not me, although…).

I almost feel angst because I'd love to start Libby on those drugs immediately. Am I one of those people who thinks a pill, as opposed to hard work, is the solution to all problems? Well, in this case, hell yes. Screw the angst. Life is hard enough. Why do I need to wait and see what animal gets bitten next before I'm allowed to give Libby medication? But, I keep all this to myself—when you visit a veterinarian's office as much as I do, the last thing you want to do is alienate the staff.

The assistant also recommends a special head halter that prevents a dog from pulling when on a leash. This sounds like it could be somewhat helpful. I'm told it's only for when Libby is being trained or walked, and should never be left on her when I'm not around. The assistant and I both agree that a traditional muzzle is not the way to go.

For the next few days, Libby gets lots of extra attention, and we work on sitting. Five days after the vet appointment, she jumps on Maggy in the backyard. I quickly pull them apart and no damage is done. At least not to them. In a domino-type effect, Lilly—my 23-pound terrier mix—decides it's her turn to jump on Maggy. They become stuck together like, well, like fighting dogs. The scuffle is loud. Fearing the sheriff two houses down is going to think I'm running a dog fighting ring or something equally ignoble, I reach in to separate them without my usual caution. Lilly bites my finger. By the next morning, it's a curved, almost inch-long cut that hurts like crazy. Even though it's a small bite, it's unlike any other cut I've ever had. (I've never been bitten by a dog before.) It's almost like the cut is in layers. (Almost exactly a month later, a red circular scar will remain, prompting the doctor when I'm at a routine checkup to ask how I got such an unusual cut on my finger.)

In the midst of the chaos, Barney is getting tall. His legs are longer than what I would expect of a pit bull from my limited experience. At work, I email (with a throbbing finger) author Ken Foster. Even though I don't know him and have never emailed an author before, I decide to give it a shot and tell him how much I enjoy his books. I attach a picture and ask if he can guess as to Barney's breed if he has time. I'm amazed when I get an email back from the author less than an hour later. His guess is American Bulldog.

I also email Amanda and show her my latest pics of Barney to ask her what she thinks. She suggests perhaps a boxer but believes there's some pit in there too.

To me, Barney looks like all of the above. And with good reason. They are all more or less connected. Many believe bulldog ancestors are what was crossed with English Terriers to get pit bulls. Others believe that the now-extinct Bullenbeisser (which functioned sort of like a shepherding dog, only they helped "herd" bulls to market) simply developed into today's pit bulls. Today's *bulldog*, on the other hand, was selectively bred to minimize aggressive traits. There are both American and English versions of today's bulldogs, with the American version having longer legs. The *boxer* was bred from Bullenbeissers and, well…something. It depends on which source you believe. Some say the boxer is a mix of Bullenbeissers and the English Bulldog. Another source claims a variety of breeds led to the boxer. All of these dogs with the alleged Bullenbeisser ancestry are part of a group a magazine I find at PetSmart the next day calls the *Bully breeds*. I like that term. It sounds so much more appealing and cuter than "pit bull."

Another reason I'm not so sure Barney is strictly pit is a story my son told me about when we were living in Greenville and his friend down the street owned a pit: Kevin was at his friend's one day. There was a rope tied to a tree. The pit jumped up and latched on. Kev went home to get a snack and back to his friend's awhile later. The dog was still hanging from the rope by his jaw. This doesn't sound like Barney behavior.

Anyway, I'm at PetSmart to look for a calming herbal remedy for Libby. I think perhaps it will keep her soothed in the evenings (when a lot of her attacks on the others take place) and maybe even serve as an alternative to pharmaceuticals. At the least, it will hopefully make the weeks till her next vet appointment less eventful. I do have some faith in herbal remedies for humans. Chamomile tea helps me sleep for example.

A jar of 30 chewable tablets—which contain chamomile flower, passion flower, thiamine mononitrate, ginger, and L-tryptophan (that soothing amino acid in turkey that is said by some to cause us to pass out in front of the television with our pants unzipped on Thanksgiving day—although, as it turns out, this is another media-generated myth because turkey does not contain enough of the tryptophan to have any sleep-inducing effects)—costs about $11.

I bring the purchase home and, after taking Libby out for a short walk, attempt to give her one of the tablets. The instructions recommend one tablet for a 50-pound dog. Libby spits it on the floor, and Barney quickly scoops it up and swallows it. I don't worry too much. He's got to be around 45 pounds at this point.

I try to give Libby another and she refuses whilst giving me the "It tastes icky" look that dogs and children usually exhibit when you try to give them something good for them. I sneak it in a table scrap and she finally swallows.

A half hour later, Libby and Barney are outside chasing each other around in circles and Barney's naturally white feet are black from running through the mud. A half hour after that, when they come in, I have to separate them because they're playing involves bumping into everything, including the other animals. Alas, the herbal remedy experiment does not seem to be off to a great start. (In contrast, when I first adopted my dog Bella, who has since passed, she had kennel cough, which quickly spread to my four other dogs at the time. Suddenly, I was living in a house in which all the dogs sounded like quacking ducks. A veterinarian suggested a small dose of Robitussin. As I was preparing a dose for Bella, Casey got a hold of the bottle and helped himself before I could grab it from him. Casey was still a bit wild in those days. About half an hour later, he was passed out cold on the couch, like a frat boy after a keg party.) A night with a break from Barney's typical energy would have been kind of nice.

In the ensuing days, I continue to try to do the best I can to get Barney exercise. In the living room, I'll throw balls or hold up a rope, which he'll chase or jump up for, respectively. Unlike the dog of my son's friend though, Barney isn't one to clamp onto a rope for long. I don't know if he is being dramatic, or is still getting used to his body (which is getting bigger by the day) but, often, after jumping up for the rope, he'll end up falling over on his side with a big thud. He also slips when he chases the balls across the tile floor and does the same sideways thud maneuver. It doesn't faze him in the slightest and he keeps on going. He's like the dog equivalent of a Tonka truck.

By the way, for those who might think this type of play is in any way cruel on my part, Barney does the same loud flop onto the floor next to me when he sits down for a snuggle, so I think it's just him learning how to handle his tall frame.

He's also *such a guy*! Casey, my Lab/hound mix, is a male too but more of a dapper, Niles Crane-kind of dog. Barney is more like the Kevin James of the dog world.

When I'm cleaning the vent of the air conditioning unit with a Q-tip, Barney comes up next to me and gives a sniff, then walks away, as if he's thinking, "Seems like kind of a waste of time to me. It's just gonna get dirty again."

When we're sitting and watching television, he'll belch. I almost feel like handing him a beer and reminding him to clean the gutters.

I guess it will take some more time, work, patience and a lot of praying that each of my dogs' distinct personalities will eventually mesh. Of course, there might also be some doggy Prozac in Libby's future. And, one beautiful day, after he is neutered, Barney will be able to go to the dog park.

Chapter 6

When I was in my late teens and early twenties, I wanted to travel the world. I loved driving, even without any particular destination. The mere act of cruising with the radio on, often with my son as sidekick, made me feel happy and in control. Weekend road trips were a pretty regular event. I loved hotels—the way they smelled, the little soaps, the ice and soda machines in the hallway, and basically the idea of being away from home.

In my early thirties, I developed what my sister and me jokingly dubbed the "homing sickness." It was at this point in our lives when we both felt like we'd rather stay home most of the time. Traveling, when necessary, began to seem disruptive and tedious to prepare for.

My sister's house is gorgeous and she put a lot of effort into making it that way. Indoors always looks like one of those dwellings photographed for magazines. Her and her husband have a pool and a great backyard too.

I have done a lot of redecorating, but for me the homing sickness was more about feeling secure, safe and comfortable. The idea of a night spent curled up with an excellent book and my animals had become more appealing than a lot of other alternatives.

Honestly, there's also some depression involved. About five years ago, when my son was 16, he was sentenced to about 10 years in prison. North Carolina tries juveniles as adults and its mandatory minimum sentencing laws are very unforgiving. Anyway, I include this information because I want people to know that, even though we sleep better at night thinking that people only go to prison if they deserve it and that, if you are in prison, you're a hardened criminal, the truth is actually much more complicated. My son, Kevin, is a sensitive, caring, good-hearted individual who made some mistakes when he was a teenager, mostly because of a drug problem. After he was sentenced, it was as if I was living with a sucking black hole of emptiness. Not coincidentally, that's when I started taking in most of the dogs and cats I have adopted. They helped fill some of the void.

Since the end of last year, when I realized I was going to turn 39 this year, I've been trying to force myself to get out of my comfort zone a bit and to take more trips. I talk to Kevin on the phone regularly and he encourages me to get out more. But, it usually involves a lot of internal dialog involving reminding myself that I'm not getting any younger and don't want to miss out on anything, followed by my argument back to myself that it's such a darn pain to drive anywhere or any of the other dozens of excuses for staying home. I'm struggling for a balance, but love taking care of my pets and wouldn't want to go back to my younger days when staying home felt restrictive.

It's probably a good thing I've changed because the animals would be kind of difficult to bring along en masse on a road trip. And, although I haven't tried yet, it seems nearly impossible to find someone to come in and care for them for more than a few days. As a group, they can be overwhelming to others. Much of the time around here, we have a dull routine going. Which can be hard for people who visit to believe because the dogs especially, and the cats to some extent, get extremely excited by company and have a hard time settling down. I do most of my socializing elsewhere—something that works out for me because a lot of time at home is spent working (writing, grading papers) or enjoying some alone (as in sans other human beings) time.

Anyway, my friend, Joy, has rescued and/or helped thousands of cats in the past six or so years. Her nonprofit, the Marley Fund, operates a safe house that shelters feline leukemia-positive cats. Joy also has a number of cats of her own. When I ask her for any advice she might have for people with multiple pets for purposes of this book, she says to be prepared to spend a lot of money—even routine care, such as regular shots and checkups, gets expensive very quickly. She ain't kidding.

Besides the shots and checkups, the dogs require regular flea prevention treatments. I use the kind that also kills ticks. Heartworm is pretty common in the south. It's expensive to treat and dangerous for the dog, so mine all take monthly heartworm prevention medication. There's also the shots, including rabies, which have to be kept up to date for the obvious reasons but also in order for them to be able to stay in a kennel in case of an emergency. Fortunately, my veterinarians (yes, I use more than one veterinary clinic—long story…) let me bring in two animals at a time.

Those are just the basics.

The cats are a whole other story. They tend to be prone to infections, including respiratory, eye and urinary tract infections. In a household with one or two cats, these illnesses would be pretty infrequent. But, when you have 14 cats, infection can be like a ping-pong ball bouncing from one animal to another. My cat population is sort of like the American baby boomer population in that it is an aging group. Because so many people would rather adopt a kitten, I usually take in older cats. That leads to all kinds of related health care issues. In the winter, for example, hundreds of dollars went to having work done on two of my cats' teeth.

One day in the summer, I noticed my cat Gwen was losing weight. I hoped she wasn't having teeth problems too. She's about 9 years old, so it wasn't out of the realm of possibility. Before I made an appointment, I tried feeding her some vitamin-fortified treats. She can eat them just fine—albeit very slowly. The other cats must have been taking all the food before she could get any. Now, I put her and her food in the bathroom alone, and she's putting on weight again rapidly. This type of easy solution at home works about 1 percent of the time, which is why I mention it. Usually, the expensive fix involving a visit to the veterinarian turns out to be the only course of action that works.

Multiple pets means expecting to be at the grocery store quite a lot too. I always seem to be running out of something. I'll stock up on dog food, only to get home and find out that the cat food bag has been knocked over and most of it, with remarkable precision, has been spilled into the water dish. Add that to tomorrow's list.

People who don't have multiple animals tend to ask me about costs. Actually, the common comment is, "I'll bet that gets expensive." Indeed. But, it's a question that can get tiresome to answer. Lately, I've taken to saying, "It depends on how fast I can run out of the store with a 20-pound bag of dog food." Ha. Ha.

I can't skip on the quality of the food either. I tried once with the cats after realizing it was past due time to better budget the household expenses (i.e. the credit card bills were starting to make me physically ill when I opened them). I bought a popular, low costing brand. In response, some of my cats went on a hunger strike and wouldn't touch the food. The ones who did eat it promptly threw it up all over the house—hard to miss, as it was very brightly colored kibble.

A large percentage of my at-home time is spent cleaning. Not that anyone could ever tell. I mean, if you walked into my house on a random day, how sparkling and spotless it is might not be the first thing that strikes you. It's not really bad like those shocking houses you see on the BBC America program, "How Clean is Your House?" in which people have let mold grow in their living room for so long that it is now a member of the family with its own television viewing preferences and everything.

But I try. And with good reason. Joy emphasizes that the cleaner the environment, the less likely bacteria can grow and cause cats to become ill. Besides bacteria, the big issues are: urine and fur. Both end up in the strangest places. As you can probably imagine, I don't even inspect my clothes for fur anymore before leaving the house because it's like trying to make sure you don't get sand in your shoes when walking on the beach. And, even though I take a shower every morning and keep my clothes hung up or in drawers, there have been a few embarrassing moments. Most recently, I was volunteering at a dog wash. I reached into my pocketbook to see if I had any change and realized it smelled like cat pee. On the inside! I keep my pocketbook hung up on a peg about five feet off the ground so I'm puzzled by this particular development, but not entirely surprised. And I'm not alone. Probably everyone who has multiple cats has had at least one experience of leaving the house and getting to their destination, such as work or a party, before realizing they're accompanied by a scent that ain't cologne, thanks to Fluffy or Socks.

Like any person taking care of numerous pets, I've learned tricks from experience to help keep everyone healthy and happy. Likewise, Carol de Olloqui, director of Marley's Cat Tales, the Marley Fund's adoption division, has some cool advice about taking care of multiple cats. She says Feliway pheromone plug-in diffusers work to help promote positive interaction in rooms inhabited by more than one cat, along with plenty of "hidey holes" where they can get away from each other (the Marley Fund offers "cat tents" for a specified donation amount, for example). She also recommends: "Lavender vanilla spray on bedding for helping to keep them relaxed, treats to reinforce good behavior—including chicken rawhides to promote chewing on appropriate things and not cords or for teething kitties." Diet is also an important consideration, with daily vitamins and L-Lysine supplements to help promote health.

Besides the practical cleaning and health information, most people in multiple pet households will have their strength tested. A lot of animal lovers end up feeling persecuted at one time or another. Some people will either intimate or come right out and accuse those who express affection for animals of caring for them more than humans. From landlords who don't allow pets to people who see squirrels and other wildlife as pests to be trapped and discarded, ours is not an animal-friendly society.

The need for strongly believing in what you are doing arises for me yet again on a sunny Saturday early on in Spring. I'm looking out my living room window. The property between my house and my neighbors' trailer is split pretty evenly. My neighbor is clearly on my half with a weed whacker, whacking away at things I'm trying to let grow (including habitat for baby birds and rabbits).

This is only the latest in a long series of inappropriate behavior on her part. I can't figure out why she's so obsessed with my property (other than to say she's a major busybody) and some small weeds and decorative grass when her backyard is a mixture of rusting metal objects and rotting trees her husband cut down with a chainsaw.

Anyway, I call my brother-in-law, John, from whom I rent the house.

"She's at it again," I tell him. Last year, when I had an extremely legitimate medical reason for not mowing my lawn and was in the process of hiring someone to mow for me, this same neighbor called John to complain.

"I can't talk to her right now. I'm too mad. I'll blow up. Can you call her and tell her to stay on her own property?" I ask John. I figure a phone call from him might be better received. It takes a lot for me to lose my temper, but, when I do, well…it isn't good.

John tells me he doesn't want to start any trouble with them because I have too many pets. Then he adds how inappropriate it is to have so many animals and how no one can possibly take care of them all.

"This isn't about me," I respond. There is no legal limit on the amount of animals I can have (outside of the township proper). "I moved out to the country so that I wouldn't be hassled."

You can never be too careful about where you live when you have pets. I've heard and read story after story from my friends and on television or in magazines about people who rescue animals and then suddenly find themselves in a horrible situation when the neighbors start complaining about noise or smell. I've received heartbreaking emails begging for help when people have only days to find new homes for their animals or have them confiscated by their local government.

I personally have seen how hard it can be to rent a place to live with even one pet, and, back on Long Island, had the unpleasant experience of having to hide pets whenever a landlord came by.

Even though local law is pretty relaxed out here, I'm still programmed from my experiences and those of others to be on the safe side. I keep my cats indoors all the time and my dogs inside most of the time. When they're outside, they're in a fenced-in area and I don't leave them out after 10 p.m. (There was a 10 p.m. noise ordinance in Greenville and I got used to following that.) This neighbor who is giving me problems is the same one with the collection of hunting dogs outside day and night that often bark or howl in unison. (Noise that I don't complain about because I don't want the animals to suffer for their owners' lack of attention.) On extra special days, I get to hear my neighbors out in their wooded property shooting at doves or dear.

My neighbor has been causing problems with me from day one. She's on my property doing yard work in the same spot I just mowed yesterday. It doesn't need yard work. If I were a man, I seriously doubt she'd be treating me this way. Plus, their front lawn is whacked to within an inch of its life. It's flat with no plants or shrubbery, only grass. I guess they think everyone's yard should look the same as theirs, making me wonder if they believe I should be piling up rusted metal objects in my backyard.

It's been almost 12 months since I quit smoking, but I'm so frustrated I go buy a pack and smoke about five cigarettes. Disgusted with myself, I run water over the remainder of the pack and throw it in the trash.

Later, John apologizes, and I accept it because he is one of my favorite people in the world, and because he's also quitting smoking, which I know from experience can make you say things less tactfully than you normally would. (Plus, a few months later, he and my sister act valiantly—like they have for animals and people countless times before—when they have trouble with their neighbors actually setting rat traps for a bunch of stray kittens. They take the one that got caught in the trap to the vet, make it clear to their neighbors that setting traps to kill kittens is not acceptable behavior, and end up keeping all four feral kittens in a spare room in their house until they can find them good homes.)

But the whole thing has still brought up feelings of defensiveness on my part. I know from firsthand and secondhand comments that some people think I'm crazy. "Weird" is how one candidate for a teaching position apparently described my living arrangements to one of the faculty members where I work. (Not that I was particularly upset because this candidate, among other unusual behaviors, brought head shot photos of himself to pass around as if he were at a casting call for actors. He didn't get the job.)

A former friend of mine put tons of money into a sailboat he couldn't really afford. Nobody makes fun of him. It's his passion, one of his favorite ways of spending time. I feel the same way about my dogs and cats, but often don't get the same benefit of the doubt he gets.

That former friend and I were briefly involved in an ill-advised attempt at being more than friends. And, if you're wondering, I don't date a whole lot because of some bad experiences. Prior to that train wreck, there was the guy I dated after a five-year break from men, whom I wrote about in a previous book, "After the Break." He started out great but turned into Mr. Apparently Has No Mental Sensor and Says Whatever Comes to Mind—not a good thing given he was seven years younger than me and at least 15 years younger maturity-wise. After Mr. I Have A Sailboat But Can't Afford My Mortgage Payment, I was seeing someone who lied about being single, and then cheated on me (and his wife) with my former friend.

So, I'm home more than a lot of people might be, and I have more time to devote to animals than those with busy social lives. I came close to falling for another man awhile back who simply said, "That shows you have compassion," after I told him about my menagerie. It was a great response. Unfortunately, he was absorbed with starting a new business and lived too far away for it to work out.

The self-pity party will pass and I'll get over it and move on, but that sense of confusion and anger about being seen as a freak for helping creatures that need help will never completely go away. In the end, after dousing my cigarettes, I write my neighbor a pretty strongly worded letter telling her to stay off my property. Then, I go outside and sit in the backyard with my animals.

Still angry, and probably withdrawing from nicotine later that night, I can't fall asleep because I'm crying so hard. This is not like me. I try to stay positive and let things like this wash off my shoulders. I'm probably an open wound because the semester is winding down. (At the end of every semester, I usually end up spending at least two days without leaving the house because I'm so exhausted physically and emotionally from 12-hour days, student complaints and excuses, grading less than stellar papers, and other job-related frustrations. In the past, I've dubbed it my end-of-the-semester nervous breakdown. But this semester has been even harder than most.) My neighbor trespassing on my property with the implied message of, "I'm going to take care of your property because you don't do a good enough job," was the last thing I needed.

I come out to the living room and sit on the couch. Sensing something is wrong, Barney crawls all over me, licking the tears off my face until I finally have to smile. Screw whatever anyone says or thinks, I decide.

I'm in it for the long haul with these furry creatures.

Chapter 7

In spite of this renewal of faith in my dedication, I realize that, back when I only lived with one dog and two cats, I too would have thought anyone with seven dogs and fourteen cats was a little fanatical. Unless you're living it though, you can't imagine how good it feels to be surrounded by so much love and such positive energy. And, amongst my friends in the animal rescue world, I'm a lightweight. Some of them have a dozen or more dogs, others more than 30 cats.

There are also practical benefits. I pointed out earlier that my dogs are often my only source of protection on trips to the store or whatever at night. There have been times at home when the electricity has gone out at 3 a.m. or I've heard some noises outside and I've felt completely safe; whereas if there were no dog around, my course of action would be to lock myself in the bathroom and cower under a blanket.

I do scare easily and it's an inherited trait. My family is a bunch of worriers. My sister and mom could be contestants for the Olympics if they had a worrying category. A typical conversation between the three of us when I go to New York usually goes something like:

"I didn't sleep well last night," my mom will say. "I kept thinking about you leaving the house for the train station and I worried about the deer."

The train departs for New York at about 3 a.m. from Rocky Mount, which is about an hour away from where I live.

"Mom, yes there are a lot of deer near where I live, but, there were also a lot when I lived in Pennsylvania. I've basically been looking out for deer when driving since 1994."

"I know, but they just come out of nowhere…"

I reiterate that, especially after 6 p.m. (deer are nocturnal), I go slow and am constantly on the lookout for the furry daredevils.

"I was worried too," my sister will then add. "But I was afraid you might get on the wrong train or something."

(This final comment is the result of my lifelong very poor sense of direction and the related fact that I got off at the wrong bus stop after my first day in kindergarten.)

And I give up because I worry about offending them when they're expressing concern for my well being. We're a fun bunch!

I know my mom well enough to know that she was at least initially worried when I told her I took in Barney. Like everyone else, she's heard the gruesome media stories about pit bulls. At the same time, I know she trusts my judgment and ability to bond with dogs, so she has not said one word to me about it even as she has probably braced herself for a "Barney ate one of my cats" phone call (or something along those lines).

At least I know my mother and sister are reassured that my dogs are keeping me safe down in North Carolina when I'm at home.

I know other people depend on their dogs in many ways too. Every time I read a book about the subject of canines, I notice that the author is in one way or another seeking to define what it is about dogs that makes them so special. Ken Foster, for example, in "The Dogs I've Met" talks about how dogs never give up. And that tenacity is another clue to why human beings who "get" dogs respond to them they way they do.

There are also other little connections. In one of my favorite parts of the book, Foster describes one of his dogs as smelling to him like fresh-baked Christmas cookies, when, to everyone else, he probably just smells like a dog. To me, Samantha smells like spring all year long—just one of the many reasons I'm enamored of her.

And, of course, there are those more cliché explanations: Dogs are loyal—a man's best friend. Canines are definitely remarkably capable of overlooking a lot of our faults and still liking us anyway. I've heard about people who never liked dogs somehow ending up with one and falling in love. Who knew having something in your home that chews on your furniture and pees on your floor, or who wakes you up at 5 a.m. every morning whining to go outside, would actually make life seem so much fuller?

I've never read or heard one simple answer. Rather, it's probably pretty complex. I do enjoy that unconditional love they give. I'm moody, and really not a morning person. I'm a lot cleaner than I used to be and care about how my house looks (and smells), but no one is ever going to refer to me as a neat freak. My sister and brother-in-law repeatedly point out my house smells like dog pee, although I beg to differ. Tidiness and order is not my forte. I'm not even sure I own an iron—to find out, I'd have to search my closets, and those I typically try not to open because it causes an avalanche of stuff. In short, I'm not an easy person to live with. Yet, the dogs never hold anything against me (although I'd of course argue any pee smell is *their* fault). My entrance into the house at the end of a day of work is always met with happiness and that sense of, "Oh man, we thought we would explode if you were gone one more minute!"

Even when I come home in a bad mood, it's hard to stay in one. I was trying to watch television one night. Barney was barking at Lilly because she wouldn't play with him. I missed every other word of what was being said on the show, until I finally shouted, "Barney, stop it!" He looked at me like he absolutely needed to convey to Lilly whatever it was he was barking. But instead, he let out this slower, almost muffled, "ah-rooo, rooo, *rooh-oooh.*" It came out as a dog's version of muttering under his breath— he just had to get in the last word. It was impossible to not laugh.

What's even more incredible is that my dogs often seem to know when they're being funny. Samantha can basically look at me to gage my mood. If she sees me smile (even if there's no other accompanying body language), she'll start wagging her tail. That sense of playfulness is something dogs and humans have in common, and helps reinforce our connections.

Samantha was only a puppy when my then-boyfriend, and 12-year-old son and I adopted her from a group of adorable black Lab puppies. Two weeks later, we were already bonded. One day, we rented a rowboat at a nearby lake. Parts of this lake were hundreds of feet deep. Anyway, we were out in the middle of it, approximately 200 feet from "shore," and Samantha all of the sudden decided to jump into the water.

It had been a long time since I'd had a dog. (After my parents divorced, I "guilted" my Mom into adopting a dog we named Swoozy when I was about 13. My mom got very attached to her and ended up keeping her after I moved into my own apartment. Swoozy lived to be about 15. She was put down because of myriad health problems.) And I never had any experience with a dog who liked to swim. It was pure instinct that made me jump out of the boat into the water after Samantha.

"Mom!" "Barb!" my son and boyfriend shouted simultaneously as I realized I was in a very deep lake and couldn't see under the surface of the water for more than a few inches. God only knows what kinds of creatures of the deep were in there with me. The image of huge snapping turtles down there staring at my feet thinking "lunchtime" flashed through my mind. Thus, seconds later, in a move that I'm sure defied gravity and, which to this day, me and Kevin still laugh about, I sort of reverse-jumped out of the lake and back into the boat. My ex-boyfriend managed to grab a hold of Samantha's collar and pull her aboard.

I'll never forget that feeling of needing to follow her into the water. It was that instinct to protect that overruled any common sense. I didn't think—I just had to save the puppy. Whether the puppy actually needed saving was another story, but it reminded me of the story my mother always tells about my sister jumping off a dock into water when she was a toddler. In less than a second my mother followed her into that lake.

Another time, when Samantha was about 4, she ran into the road as a car was coming. Again, without thinking, I ran out after her. It was a residential road and the car wasn't going very fast, but incidents like that always serve to remind me how really, truly attached I am to this dog. There is some indefinable bond between myself and her— it's part maternal, part friendship, and part something else I can't quite explain. That "friendship" feeling is something that a lot of dog people probably identify with. I've met many people walking their dog(s) while I'm walking mine. And when we stop to talk, I often learn how dedicated the person is to their canine. There's something magical about these interspecies friendships. When you're communicating with an animal, it makes you feel more connected to the world around you.

And every time I tell any of my animals that I love them, there is always some reaction. I remember the first time I told Samantha—she started licking my face with great enthusiasm. It's true of the cats too. If I say, "I love you" to a cat, they might purr, or rub against me, or simply blink their eyes—but there is always some kind of discernible response.

Still, while it's easy to think of animals as Disney characters with only good intentions, they can be subject to basic instincts, which aren't always so Disney-like. When I go to work or even run out for an hour or two to do an errand, I always separate the dogs. Since Barney's arrival into the mix, I've had to rearrange things a bit. Now, Libby goes in the fenced-in yard. Barney gets the living room and kitchen. Casey, Samantha and Lilly go in the bedroom. Maggy wants to stay out with Barney, which isn't optimal but I guess they get along okay. I've tried to keep her in the spare bedroom, but she runs away from me. They all act like my bedroom is the Ritz-Carlton, but the spare bedroom is apparently more like Rikers Island.

Maggy (the spitz mix) and Lilly (small, terrier mix) have the strangest relationship. Sometimes they play together like best friends. Maybe every three or four months they'll get into a real spat. Maggy is about 30 pounds. Lilly is about 23 (although she could probably stand to lose a few pounds). No one ever ends up bleeding, but it's not fun to watch when they're rolling around, tussling and growling like rabid raccoons.

A friend of mine was bitten several times on the arm once trying to break up a fight between her dogs, so (with the exception of the Lilly/Libby/Maggy incident after the sheriff visit) I know better. When they fight, I run for a cup of water and toss it on them. That's usually effective. Most of the time, they're both already wet from each others' saliva, but it doesn't seem like the teeth of either of them has actually made it past their furry coats, let alone broken the skin. I, on the other hand, am a wreck, shaking like Jell-o afterwards and almost always speechless when—

as few as five minutes later—they play together as if nothing happened.

Another reality is that I need to develop some kind of rescue plan. All the newsletters from various animal organizations suggest it, especially after the horrors pets and their people experienced because of Hurricane Katrina. I don't live in a flood plain—which is comforting given that a lot of Eastern North Carolina was badly flooded by Hurricane Floyd in 1999 (a year before I moved to the area). Still, I start to think about how I'd get 14 cats into cages and 7 dogs onto leashes. And then what would I do with them once everyone is "gathered?" I own a Geo Metro. Circus clowns who specialize in squeezing large groups of humans into a car would probably say, "Sorry, there's no way all those animals will fit." So, I keep hoping for the best—and occasionally consider building an ark. A few months ago, my sister emailed me. She said that someone at work told her flood plains were changing because of global warming. After hearing that, she had a dream that my house got flooded and I had to get all the animals out. I emailed her back immediately asking how exactly we did this in her dream—just in case it was a legitimate idea I could incorporate in real life. I think she thought I was kidding, so she didn't respond. I wasn't.

In May, something happens that makes the fights between Maggy and Lilly—or anything I've seen Libby do—seem like child's play. It's sort of a long story. Barney has been continuing to drive me and the animals crazy with all his energy. I haven't been able to take him anywhere except the veterinarian for two main reasons:

1) His continuing stomach troubles. It might be awkward to be out in public somewhere and have Barney suddenly hunch over to go to the bathroom and make his loud, screaming noise in the process. While he doesn't make the noise each time he goes to the bathroom anymore,

he hasn't stopped completely. And, I can't imagine what people would think of a screaming bully dog in the park or pet store.

2) His diarrhea has decreased, but not completely gone away either. Thus, I still have to wait before he can be neutered. If his behavior at home is any indication, he would try to mount other dogs (he also tries to mount some of my cats) that we come across.

Eventually, I decide that I need to get him out in spite of those issues. Whenever I've brought in a new dog in the past, I immediately started taking them on car trips with me (if it's cool enough to leave them in the car if I'm going into a store); or to PetSmart, the park, the dog park, etc. In the process, they learn all kinds of things, including how to walk on a leash, how to wait quietly in the car until I come back, and simply that there are other people in the world. Barney has been missing all of these lessons, so on May 14 at around 6 p.m., I take him to the agricultural center. There's a lot of land, a pond, trail walks, and usually—after the center is closed on a weekday—not too many people are around.

As soon as I park the car and open the door, Barney jumps out. From his body language, I can tell that he simultaneously wants to go in every direction at once. His head is facing one way, his front legs are turning to the side, but his back legs appear ready to head in the other direction. It's hard to know exactly what the first six months of his life were like. But, since he arrived in January, his whole world has pretty much been the inside of my house and my backyard.

He now truly looks like a kid who has just been let into a theme park for the first time, without any prior knowledge that theme parks even existed. At first, I can't walk a step without him running around and me having to spin around to unravel myself from the leash. Then, we get into a rhythm and he walks a few feet ahead with this jaunty bounce in his step. His head is up and so is his tail. I can tell he's thinking, *"This is great!"* He is not just walking—he is PRANCING! I'm so tempted to let him off the leash to run around, but there are still a few people coming out of the agricultural building. We walk down to the pond. Other than being somewhat surprised when he steps into the water, he doesn't appear interested in the idea of swimming, so we turn around and take a long walk around the grounds.

After we leave the park, I decide to stop at the dollar store to buy some pain reliever for a headache. It takes about five minutes just to get out of the car because Barney is determined that he's going to come with me. I've got a hold on the leash but he pushes with all his front muscles when I try to open the door a crack and he jumps out before I can. He immediately panics because this is a full parking lot, with people coming and going (unlike the almost empty lot at the agricultural center). I try to stay calm, but am terrified he's going to pull his head out of his collar and end up running loose. Penny (Corgi mix) did this on a shopping trip once when I first adopted her, and I ended up chasing her into an alley (fortunately, she didn't run the other way, which was an incredibly busy street) before I finally got a hold of her.

I grab Barney and have to lift him back into the car, keeping one hand on him until the door is almost completely closed. Then I slip out my hand and shut the door. He looks terrified that he's being abandoned.

"Barney, I'll be right back," I tell him, wondering what the man who has been sitting in the car next to us this whole time is thinking.

When I return with my purchase a few minutes later, Barney is staring anxiously out the window. He sees me headed in his direction and his tail spins like a helicopter blade. When I'm back in the car, he puts his head on my lap and stays that way for most of the ride home. Except for the fact that he's drooling on me, it's an improvement from the night he first turned up when he howled like a banshee all the way to the animal hospital.

The next day my friend Amanda sends me an email with a link to a newspaper story about a 3-year-old North Carolina boy killed by a dog. The first line of the story identifies the dog as a pit bull. She tells me to take a look at the comments from readers at the end of the story.

"It'll break your heart to see how…much people hate pit bulls," she writes.

By the time I visit the site, there are about 90 comments. She's right. Someone has posted the usual myths about pit bulls, including the locking jaw one, as if they're fact and follows with the ominous, "They are not to be trusted."

I leave a comment stating that I looked for a picture of the dog, found one at another news site and ask others to see if it is indeed a pit bull. Someone has posted a story about a woman who was suddenly killed by her pit bull for no reason, so I post another message.

"Before passing on stories on this blog, it would probably be a good idea to include the source so that we can all judge whether these stories are legitimate," I write.

Another user, whom I'll call Angry Dog Hater (although he doesn't sound like a big fan of humans either), and who has already left a number of anti-pit bull comments, makes snide comments about my posts. He also derides the posts of others defending dogs or attempting to post truthful information about bully breeds to clear up the misconceptions.

I decide, because I'm a communication instructor and this is how we think, that I'm going to read all the comments posted so far and divide them up into three categories: pro pit bull, pit bull negative, and neutral.

Almost immediately I realize this process is not going to be easy. For one, there are also comments that are negative about dogs in general, and comments that seem to be both pit bull negative and positive at the same time. Also, after comment #18, a considerable number of posts are from the Angry Dog Hater, who has commandeered the blog for some kind of anti-human, anti-dog rant that takes away from any kind of meaningful discussion. But, from just the small sample of the first 18 comments, there are:*

   (*Some of the comments were more detailed and harder to put in a category, so, in those cases, I went by the predominant theme of the message.)

•1 negative comment about dogs in general,

•8 pit bull negative comments including the following two,

—"This yet another incident involving a Pit Bull and this one results in the death of a small child. I'm sure there will be those that say the dogs are friendly, and great with their family, etc., etc. but I just don't buy it." [sic]

—"why is this society even allowing pit bulls to continue to be bred? is still see them advertised in the pet section of the newspaper. makes zero sense." [sic]

•6 comments that fall into the broad category of neutral and/or proposing solution to stop dog attacks and/or expressing sorrow for the victim.

•There's one comment I don't even know where to place, so it gets its own category,

—"I guess pitbulls can be mean but my neighbor has one and he is the sweetest dog he didnt even know me and he got in my yard one day and came up on my deck started licking me and playing with my dog! I guess if he wasnt used to kids or people he would attack for no reason." [sic]

•2 pro pit bull comments,

—"My sympathy goes out to the family. Dogs attack based on how they are trained by their owners. I grew up with Pit Bulls and they were not aggressive dogs because they were not trained to be aggressive or fighters. I understand there are some/certain things that can trigger a dog's reaction, but

NOT ALL pit bulls are mean. Any dog can attack, no matter what bread." *[sic]*

—"Any dog can attack. Everyone is just quick to jump to the assumption that all dog attacks involve pitbulls…Yes I once felt the same way about pit bulls until I actually owned one and to this day she is one of my babies, even sleeps in the bed with my daughter." *[sic]*

In spite of what Angry Dog Hater spews in his comments, of course people can love dogs and stick up for them *and* simultaneously realize it is horrible that a child was killed. And I don't think that any dog that kills a child should be kept alive, so I'm not defending this particular dog.

I do want to know if it's really a pit bull, so I email the picture to a contact address at the Real Pit Bull Web site. I'm having a hard time seeing a resemblance to any pit pictures I've seen and it's even harder because the picture only shows the dog's head and only from the side.

The response email states, "The dog looks like a Pit Bull or pit mix to me."

Darn. It's so odd. I've so recently been learning about pit bulls causing human deaths being so extremely rare; how has this actually happened within about 90 miles of my home? I badly wanted it to not be a pit or even a pit mix at all – to get a "If that's a pit, I'm a flying monkey"-kind of response.

Only one day later, I witness the most serious fight between two of my dogs that I have ever seen. Maybe the best way to explain is through the text of an email I sent to Amanda a few days after it happened:

The strangest thing happened…Casey does not like Barney. I think it's because Barney is an un-neutered male…Anyway, they got into a fight the other night -- it was the first one that involved actual contact. (Casey has barked/growled at Barney before but never bitten him.) I was weighing Casey to see which Advantix I should use on him and I guess he felt cornered because Barney got too close to him and the next thing they were biting and rolling all over the place. It took me about 10 minutes to get them apart and I actually ended up out of breath--feeling like I'd just jogged a mile. It was really hard because I'd just get Casey's jaws off Barney's head and then Barney would dodge around me and fly back at Casey. (I kept thinking about all those things I read about pit bulls not wanting to give up a fight.) I threw water on them, I tried to get a chair in between them. It was awful. Finally, I threw a blanket over Barney and dragged him out into the sunroom. Casey ended up with one cut on his face, which no one would ever know was there (it's hidden under his fur) unless they knew to look. Barney, on the other hand, has about five cuts on his head (his short fur doesn't give him too much protection, I guess). Since then, I've had to keep them separated, which isn't easy. Today, they were sniffing at each other through the sunroom door, which was open a couple of inches [but held shut by a chain lock], *but they were acting like nothing ever happened. Just looking at each other like* hey, what's up? *The strange thing to me is that I had no idea Casey had that in him. He's this...gentle lab mix and he beat the heck out of my "pit bull." By the way, Barney is okay. None of his cuts were deep enough to need stitches or anything.*

Barney spends the next couple of weeks looking as if he went a few rounds with Mike Tyson as his bite marks almost heal and then Libby insists on licking them, slowing down the recovery process. His "wounds" are all on his head and neck. His body is okay. It could be a lot worse. Even that little mark I got from Lilly biting me by accident was like no other cut I've ever had. A significant wound from a dog would be very serious. I tell Amanda and no one else because I don't want anyone to think it's somehow Barney's fault—I'm now well associated with people's tendency to blame the pit bull. Also, I don't want people to think it happened because I have too many animals. I know of at least three people who "only" have two dogs that have ended up fighting with each other, so I don't think household number is the only or overriding factor in dog fights.

It takes about a week for me to shake off the shock of what happened. It was so violent, so brutal and so unexpected. In my head, I keep seeing Casey's jaw locked on Barney's head. And them rolling around. And me pulling Barney and Casey apart. And Barney flying right back at Casey, determined not to let the fight end. And it makes that article about the little boy who was killed seem so much more real. I mean, there's a difference between knowing intellectually that something awful took place and actually empathizing with it on a deeper level.

I search for another article to see if I can find out more about what happened. According to that article, the boy lived in a house on a military base. His parents went out and left him with a babysitter. The sitter had a friend who came over and brought along the dog. When the parents came home, the dog was on top of the boy. He died on the way to the hospital. How absolutely horrific and sad and awful. I feel like an idiot for being so cavalier as to make comments defending pit bulls on the news site's article. My intentions to get the truth about pit bulls out to the public were well meaning, but I chose the wrong forum.

In retrospect, even though the fight between Casey and Barney seemed as if it came out of the blue, I reassessed the situation and figured out that there were warning signs and that I did a number of things that contributed to the fight. I should never have weighed Casey with the bathroom door open because it required picking up Casey and lifting him onto the scale in the corner of the room. This allowed Barney to follow us in, and probably made Casey feel cornered and vulnerable.

Before their big fight, I had eaten in front of them every day and they would compete with each other for any crumbs of scraps that fell (which sounds kind of Dickensian, but they're all well fed and I've been eating in front of my dogs without issue for years). That led to a lot of growling from Casey in warning to Barney. I never thought Casey would seriously go after Barney. I realize that I can't be careless like that anymore. While for me, it's just lunch, for them it caused a whole lot of intense feelings.

After a couple of weeks, I let them gradually spend longer periods of supervised time together in the same room, being careful not to repeat any of the previous mistakes. (Unfortunately, in spite of my being more alert and ready to separate them at the first sign of a problem, months later they get into a worse fight in the blink of an eye. I decide it's best to keep them completely separated all the time. When Barney's outside, Casey has the run of the house, etc.)

When all is said and done, we can gain a lot and learn a lot from dogs. But, maybe the most important thing to remember while we're all sharing our lives with each other is that canines have their own instincts and behavioral patterns. We can and should celebrate the similarities and differences between ourselves and canines that make us smile or feel safe or otherwise enhance our lives. But, we should never forget to respect how complex those differences can be.

But, as it turns out, the story didn't end there. In July, I'm in my office after teaching class. I'm preparing some things for class the next day, but have Barney on the brain. I do a random search for images on Google of pit bulls. I just want to see some pictures because they can be such pretty dogs. One of the images that comes up is very familiar. It's the photo of the dog that accompanied the story about the boy killed by a dog—the same exact news picture I emailed to The Real Pit bull to ask for confirmation that it was a pit. Only it's labeled as an Associated Press photo of a 3-year-old pit bull named Sassy belonging to Tom Garner, "a leading pit bull breeder" in North Carolina.

Wait…what?! My adrenaline starts pumping and I do a search for the dog attack story showing that same picture. On the abc11.com Web site, there's the headline "Child dies after dog attack" and underneath is the same picture with a tiny caption I missed the first time around. It says, "Authorities say North Carolina has become something of a center for pit bull breeding." So, inasmuch as identifying the breed or breed mix of the actual dog involved in the attack on the child, I'm back to square one because there are apparently no pictures available of that dog. I guess that's why the news Web site chose to use an AP Style photo of another dog—a pit bull named Sassy who likely has never hurt anyone. A photo that probably a lot of people in addition to myself thought was the dog involved in the attack. Wondering whether the breeder of Sassy knows how his dog's picture was used, I look for his Web site, locate an address and email him, but he never emails me back.

Two days later, I take Barney to the veterinarian. He is now at 61 pounds and counting. He needs another shot so he can stay at the kennel in August when I go to New York for a few days. The veterinarian cannot believe how big he is and keeps telling me what a great job I've done. In truth, maybe I helped, but most of the credit goes to Barney for hanging in there and never losing heart during his long and sometimes painful recovery.

"He's a fighter," I tell her.

And I mean that in the absolute best sense of the term.

Chapter 8

If I repeatedly mentioned the local fenced-in dog park in this book (and I think we know I did), I hope you'll forgive me. It was a long time coming, and I never thought our community (not terribly dog friendly from what I'd seen previously) would open one. But they did. And it's great.

When I lived in Shippensburg, Pennsylvania, while going to college, there was never any problem finding a place to exercise my dog, Samantha. There were plenty of times when the university's football and baseball fields were empty, and I'd take her out and play Frisbee with her. Another part of campus, which was not well known and, thus, an amazing hidden treasure, had a field and a stream—a great place for her to run and swim. It was less than 10 minutes from where I lived. There were plenty of other places too. About 10 miles away was a state park where my son and I could also go for long walks on trails with Samantha off leash.

It has been much more difficult to find similar places in Greenville, North Carolina, especially as the number of dogs I have has grown. Walking them around the block as I used to do when I lived in town never seemed like good enough exercise for them. Plus, try walking four dogs (I *only* had four dogs back then) at one time. Any time a person or another dog crossed our path, my dogs would all go nuts and we'd become a tangled mass of leash, fur and disoriented human. (By the way, only after I moved from Greenville did I find out that the city has a limit of three dogs per household. Oops!)

I lived two blocks away from a park for five years. The park is decent-sized. There's a tennis court, a baseball field, two playgrounds, and some surrounding open fields. But it got full of people in the afternoons and stayed that way for most of the day. So, one morning, my dogs and I headed to the park at 7 o'clock. It appeared empty, so I let them off their leashes and they gleefully started to play. Out of the corner of my eye I saw a man and his son, who was about 7, approaching.

Maggy, looking like the ball of fluff she is, ran up to the little boy and stood on her hind legs, putting her paws on the boy's chest. I apologized and started trying to round the dogs up as the child warned me that I should train Maggy not to jump up on people. I am *so* not a morning person, yet I came to the park at 7 a.m. so I wouldn't have to worry about encountering people and whether my dogs would mind their manners. But, the boy and his father were good-natured enough, so I thanked the child for the advice and moved on.

The next day, I started going to the park at 6:30 a.m. I quickly realized that people who worked at some of the buildings in the vicinity of the park were coming to work at that time. They did not appear thrilled to be greeted by my furry, tail-wagging troupe. One woman wouldn't get out of her car till I had Casey back on a leash. I was starting to feel like the only person in the entire town who not only actually liked dogs but was not actively terrified of or repulsed by them.

I decided our park trips would need to be at the time of the day when people were probably either still sleeping or just getting up. The perfect time to go would be when it was still a little dark yet light enough to see, I reasoned.

The next morning at around 5:30 the dogs were running around happily until a man, who was maybe 50 years old or so, approached. I tried to gather the dogs, but they were much more interested in this strange person entering their play area. Why he decided to walk directly toward us when there were plenty of other routes he could have taken to bypass us completely, I'll never know, especially since he immediately became angry when the dogs ran over to him. He started waving a shiny, metal object, which I couldn't see very well—it appeared to be either a comb or a knife. I yelled to him to please stop waving his arms around and to stand still so I could get the dogs to come to me.

"They don't bite," I kept shouting, doubting he could hear me over all the yelling he was doing at my animals. They were not in any way acting in a threatening manner toward him. I think they were extremely curious about this stranger and his odd movement.

This all seemed to go on in slow motion for about three hours, although it was probably more like two or three minutes. Somehow, I got everyone back on their leashes and started heading for home.

"I'm calling the police," the man yelled with an odd combination of enmity and glee. "You're going to jail!"

"It's 5:30 in the morning!" I yelled back—neither of us spewing forth any dialog that would have qualified us for even an amateur debate team.

Anyway, the man actually followed me and the dogs to my house and almost onto my lawn until I told him that if he didn't get away from my property it would be me who called the police on him.

About 15 minutes later, a police officer showed up at my door and told me to make sure to keep my dogs on leashes in the future.

I started taking them to the park at night after 9 o'clock when it had cleared out again. We'd go onto the empty tennis court, and I'd close the gate so they could run around inside (I made sure to clean up any accidents). This continued to work pretty well until one night when three men told me to leave the park immediately because there was "some guy running around with a shotgun." I have no idea why they were there given that they knew it wasn't safe, but mostly I concerned myself with rounding up the dogs and getting the heck out of the park.

After that, I completely gave up. Having been threatened with both arrest and potentially being shot at made me loathe to find out what might happen next. Since, apparently, there was no time of the day whatsoever when the park would ever be completely empty, and, since I didn't want to make my dogs wear bulletproof vests and only go out accompanied by a team of high powered attorneys, I decided we'd all stay home and watch television. I thought things would be better when I moved into a house in the country with three acres, but only a small portion of that is fenced in and the dogs would head straight to the road when I tried letting them off leash outside of that area.

So, it was a cause for much rejoicing when a student in my class mentioned one day at the end of the winter 2007 semester that there was a new dog park in Greenville.

It is so nice to be able to go somewhere I don't have to deal with people who don't like dogs. With some exceptions, most people there are accepting of a variety of dog behaviors that seem to make other people irate.

Every single town should have a dog park. There are innumerable benefits. Most obviously, the dogs gets exercise, which leads to happier dogs *and* people. Sometimes I'll look around and think about how all these dogs who are running off leash releasing enormous amounts of pent-up energy might very well otherwise take out the same energy on furniture and other household objects were they stuck in houses or apartments all day.

Also, people at the dog park are exposed to different breeds and a variety of mixes, and can get to see the truth about bully breeds and other dogs.

For us "dog people," it's great to be around other people like us. It can be awkward when I'm with friends who don't have dogs, but who have young children. When they tell a story about something their kids did and I counter with something my dogs did that reminds me of their story, you can almost see them do a quick scan around to make sure there are no sharp objects near me, lest I completely lose my mind. Or, I can see their shock and I realize that they don't so much appreciate me comparing their beloved, brilliant children to my pets. So it's nice to socialize with people who understand.

Personally, I think everyone should adopt a dog. Well, everyone who would provide a good home. I know people who have valid reasons for not having dogs. There are others, though, who I believe would benefit from having a dog, or cat, or both in their lives. They are animal people waiting to happen. They just don't know it yet.

They also don't know what they're missing. Sometimes, when I'm at the dog park, I feel like the coolest, most together person in the world. I'll show up with my sunglasses (which, while it might seem like an aesthetic decision, is because there's a lot of dirt and fur flying through the air, which can turn my eyes bright red) and a cup of iced-tea (with a spillproof cap), and my laptop computer. I'll let whichever dogs are with me off their leashes. They'll be the good dogs—the ones who run around but steer clear of the more aggressive dogs that garner disapproving looks from the other people at the park. I'll smugly sit back on one of the benches and answer my email (I pirate a wireless Internet connection from a nearby apartment complex) or work on a writing project, such as this book.

Then again, on occasion I wouldn't mind a trap door that would let me slip out quickly and quietly before people can make the connection between me and the dogs I'm with. For better or worse, people do attribute their dogs' behavior to their owners— something I was painfully aware of when I took Casey and Libby (this was prior to her jumping on the other dog) to the park one day. Libby kept running to me for protection because the other dogs were ganging up on her. Casey kept going to a corner of the fence and barking at the squirrels on the other side. I can't emphasize enough how much Casey dislikes squirrels. He was very upset about the ones running up and down a tree and ignoring him; his whole body was shaking. When he gets that way, you can almost hear him thinking, "Oh, there they are again. Running around and looking all...*squirrelly!*"

At one point another dog came over, like, "What are you looking at man?"

Casey just kept barking at the squirrels. The other dog took a look, lost interest and wondered away, like, "Squirrels man, what can you do?" If the dog could have shrugged, he would have.

It made me happy that Casey and Libby were dogs because I have the feeling if they were two kids and we were on a playground, someone would have recommended family counseling.

Anyway, you can make a big difference for dogs by getting an off leash dog park established in your area if you don't already have one. Hey, if people managed to get one in Greenville—the town in which an old lady nearly had an aneurism from screaming at Casey when he ran across her lawn during an attempted escape from my yard back in his more rebellious days (no he didn't relieve himself or anything, just ran across it in a matter of maybe 10 seconds at the most and she was *inside* her house at the time but yelled at him through the window)—you can probably get a dog park anywhere. Sites, such as dogplay.com, provide information about how.

There are also a number of other ways to help bully breeds and other dogs:

•Break the chains.

Because dogs confined to chains or ropes for most of their existence can become dangerous, a good first step in your community is getting an anti-tethering ordinance passed. As mentioned in Chapter 5, the Humane Society offers a step-by-step kit explaining how to get such laws on the books in your area. For the kit and more information, visit: humanesociety.org/dogchainingkit.

These laws usually aren't passed overnight, so another short-term option comes through Dogs Deserve Better. This nonprofit with an extensive history of helping dogs will send information to addresses of homes that have dogs tethered or otherwise continually confined outdoors. The information is designed to encourage these owners to consider bringing their dog(s) inside at least part of the time or finding the dog(s) a new home. This is a good option for people who want to do something but don't want to directly confront neighbors or others about mistreatment of their animals. (And, yes, I supplied my neighbors' address to Dogs Deserve Better. They didn't bring their dogs inside but they did start stepping up their care for the animals.)

• Get dogs out of the dog house and into the home.

Tamira Ci Thayne, founder of Dogs Deserve Better, notes on the site (www.dogsdeservebetter.com) that most dogs her organization rescues are able to adjust fairly easily and often can be housetrained within one to two weeks. (By the way: Thayne's name translates loosely to "Peaceful Dog Warrior"—she changed it legally from Tammy Grimes in the summer of 2008.)

Still, being indoors can be a whole new world for an animal. Fear and aggression can take longer to subside. Dogs Deserve Better posts an article by Debby Dobson, the owner of "Good Dog!" Animal Behavior in Arizona, on the Web site. The article describes the steps to helping an outdoor dog make the transition to indoor.

Dobson, who has worked with dogs for over 20 years, states that **patience, consistency** and **balance** are key. A frightened dog might cower, growl, snap, hide, put its ears back or fold its tail between its legs. Dobson says this is where patience comes in, including the ability to be able to understand how "overwhelming" the indoor environment might seem.

It took days for some of my dogs to get used to household noises (such as the washing machine) that I don't even notice anymore.

Most dogs new to the indoor environment will probably want to get into everything. A lot like toddlers, dogs will want to put everything in their mouths. Put your precious objects up high! Then go get a stepstool and raise them up another 6 to 12 inches or so.

Consistency, says Dobson, includes having "regularly scheduled events a dog can count on and look forward to" such as an afternoon walk followed by a treat. I wholeheartedly agree. Whenever there's a change in my schedule, my dogs tend to be on edge and more likely to have accidents indoors, get in the garbage or otherwise make mischief.

And—although it might be tempting to smother a dog with affection to try to make up for what they've missed—Dobson warns against forgetting to also be consistent in correcting negative behaviors.

"Far better to say 'NO!' every now and again than to have a dog who doesn't understand acceptable boundaries and behavior," Dobson writes.

Finally, balance can prevent overloading a dog with too much stimulation at once. Dobson suggests focusing on getting a dog used to walking on a leash without trying to combine other socializing. Once the dog becomes acclimated to the leash, then take another step, such as bringing the dog somewhere it will meet new people and dogs. When meeting other dogs, start with a nose to nose contact and praise the dog for positive encounters. Remove the dog from the situation at the first sign of any aggression and try again later.

"Because their emotional growth was 'stunted,' these dogs vacillate between fear/aggression and a huge outpouring of affection that can sometimes border on neediness. The goal is twofold: to help them overcome their fears and to simultaneously boost their confidence," Dobson advises.

I'd also add that staying calm is important. I read recently about a dog that was almost put to sleep because its owners thought it was acting aggressively. Turned out the dog was displaying a submissive grin meant to show, "Hey, I'm all about cooperating with you," but which was taken as, "Hey, I'm about to sink my teeth into you." In other words, avoid the temptation to think that a dog can't be rehabilitated because that animal might be trying its hardest to fit in even though we don't always pick up on those efforts or signs.

By the way, Dogs Deserve Better is a Pennsylvania-based organization that re-homes between 700–1,000 dogs annually and boasts representatives and members in states all over the country. The group is planning a rescue, rehabilitation and training center for dogs rescued from lives on chains or in pens.

• **Bully breeds on the Net.**

Web sites can be great clearing houses, full of facts about pits and other dogs. But, unless someone is searching for information on the topic, they probably won't come across these sites. Take every opportunity to use the Internet to provide easy-to-access positive images of bully breeds and help increase traffic to established pages. For example, set up your own Web page with pictures of your dog(s) and links to various positive pit sites. Also, you can email addresses of positive pit bull video to everyone you know and ask them to forward to everyone they know. For example: www.youtube.com/watch?v=vL1trl1FMUw is the link to a great video about pitties.

• **Be a news media watchdog:**

Most local television news stations and newspapers are interested in what their viewers have to say, at least partially because they don't want ratings to go down. But they won't know how you feel unless you contact them. Email, phone or write letters to your local news organization(s) whenever you hear questionable reports about pit bulls. Be polite, but inform local reporters that they need to be educated about pit bulls so as to prevent furthering myths about these dogs. Also be brief. Usually news organizations, which are often pressed for time, respond better to concise requests than lengthy ones.

You can also contact your local newspaper and television station(s), and ask them to consider doing news reports that educate the public about dogs in general. For example: *Covering how to act around loose dogs in order to prevent attacks; and how to integrate children and dogs within a household.*

Also, don't be afraid to congratulate and thank news organizations when they offer animal-friendly programming. My local news station is admirable for the work it does to spread the message that dogs (and children!) should not be left in a parked car for even a minute or two on a hot day.

• Be a good role model whether you have two legs or four.

There's often nothing more persuasive than personal experience. Therefore, a friendly, sociable bully breed dog can go a long way toward helping change people's minds about these dogs.

The Pit Bull Rescue Central Web site offers particularly good advice: "Every negative incident involving a pit bull adds to their reputation and jeopardizes our right to own these great dogs. Keep your pit bull out of trouble!"

•Help ban breed bans.

Now that I have a dog that may be a pit bull, but is definitely a bully breed, where I can live in the future is limited to communities that don't have bully breed bans. I even worry about driving through strange towns on the way to somewhere else with Barney in my car. What if I got pulled over and there was a ban I didn't know about? What if my car broke down in an area with a ban and Barney was with me? Would he be confiscated? I can barely stand to think about what could go wrong.

At a discussion of whether to adopt a pit bull ban in the City of Jacksonville, Arkansas, a local veterinarian pretty strongly stated opposition. The minutes from the City Council meeting include the comments of this veterinarian, Dr. Lee Misak: "He stated that in general he is against banning any breed of dog, adding that the American Humane Society, American Animal Hospital Association, American Veteran Medical Association, National Animal Control Association, National Animal

Interest Alliance, American Kennel Club, and the United Kennel Club do not favor banning of any specific breed. He acknowledged that there are two fractions [SIC] of pit bulls, those that make excellent pets and those that are fighters. He stated that the average veterinarian would claim that 90% of the pit bulls seen in a veterinarian office are friendly, adding that he is aware of the other end of the scale regarding very aggressive pit bulls."

Later, during that same meeting, the council voted to adopt the ban anyway.

Bans are ridiculous, and I'd encourage the public at large to not support community bans on any breed of dog. There are other, better alternatives if dog bites or aggressive dogs are a problem. I would also recommend people doing what they can to prevent new bans or help have bans repealed where they live. Dog prohibition has done more harm than good for numerous animals.

A better alternative is educating the public about animal care. According to the American Veterinary Medical Association, "Responsible pet ownership and education have been shown to be the key factors in reducing the number of (dog) bites that occur in a community." In its online Journal, the AVMA recommends targeting "chronically irresponsible owners."

According to Wikipedia, there are bans in certain cities/counties in the following states: Colorado, Florida, Iowa, Kansas, Maryland, Missouri, New York, Ohio, Oklahoma, Tennessee, Utah and Washington.

I thought it would be easy to confirm the Wikipedia information from an official list at a more traditional source. Boy, was I wrong. After a lot of searching, the only source I was able to find with what appeared to be a pretty complete and up-to-date list was Understand-a-bull.com. According to this site, the list of states with city and/or county bans is longer than the one on Wikipedia. The only states that don't have any such breed legislation are: Alaska, Delaware, Maine, Massachusetts, Nevada, New Hampshire, New Jersey, Rhode Island, Vermont, Virginia and Wyoming. That's only 11 out of 50 states!

What are some of the local laws like? Well, in Miami-Dade County, Florida, if a dog "substantially conforms to" a pit bull breed dog (and wasn't registered in the county prior to 1989), the owner is fined $500 and court action is taken to remove the animal from the county. It's an outrageous amount of money that most people can't easily afford. The wording of the law makes it dangerous too. The law doesn't simply state that specific pit bull breeds are banned. It says that dogs appearing close enough to that type of dog can be banned. Which means that, even if Barney isn't technically a pit bull, he still likely isn't welcome in Miami-Dade County. Overall, this seems less like justice and more like a case of ignorance and fear morphing into legislation. Miami-Dade even has a post on the county's Web site providing information on how neighbors and others can turn in someone for possession of a "pit bull dog." Yes, indeed, big brother is watching you! Oh, and be careful not to tick off your neighbors, lest your beloved family pet looks a little too much like a bully breed dog.

Even bans that seem sensible or reasonable on the surface cause their share of damage. In Jacksonville, Arkansas, the ordinance that went into effect in July of 2007 required all pit bulls, predominantly pit bull mix and most bulldogs to be microchipped and neutered prior to the date of the institution of the ban. (As noted earlier, bulldogs may look like pits, but the American Bulldog and English Bulldog are **not** pit bull breeds, and English Bulldogs have been bred selectively for non aggression, increasing the "**what the F!*$?**" factor of this particular banning instance.) New dogs of these types are not allowed to be adopted in the community. It took a number of attempts at contacting different departments in Jacksonville, but I was finally able to obtain a copy of the exact wording of the ordinance, which starts:

1. **Ban** *It shall hereafter be unlawful for any person, firm, or corporation to keep, own, or harbor within the City limits any of the following breeds of dog(s):*

a) *Stafford Bull Terrier;*
b) *American Pit Bull Terrier;*
c) *American Bull Dog;*
d) *Dogs of mixed breed or of other breeds than the above-listed whose breed is known as Pit Bull, Bull Dogs, or Pit Bull Terrier;*
e) *Any breed being a predominate breed of a Stafford Bull Terrier, an American Pit Bull Terrier, Bull Dog, or any mixed breed thereof; and,*
f) *Any dog whose sire or dam is a dog of a breed which is defined as a banned breed of dog under this Ordinance.*

2. **Registration** *Any owner, keeper, or harborer of a dog listed above will have Thirty (30) days after passage and publication of this Ordinance to register the animal with Jacksonville Animal Control pursuant to the following criteria:*

a) *The animal was licensed prior to the effective date of this Ordinance;*
b) *The owner, keeper, or harborer shall provide proof of rabies vaccination;*
c) *The owner, keeper, or harborer must be at least Twenty-one (21) years of age;*
d) *The owner, keeper, or harborer shall, at his/her own expense, have the animal spayed or*

neutered and/or shall present to the Jacksonville Animal Control documentary proof from a licensed veterinarian that a sterilization procedure has been performed on said animal. An owner of such a prohibited animal may be exempted from the spay or neuter requirement. To obtain such an exemption, documentation must be provided from a licensed veterinarian stating that a spay or neuter procedure would put the animal's life at-risk at that time, but the documentation must specify a timeframe within which the sterilization procedure can be completed;

e)   The owner, keeper, or harborer shall bring the animal to the Jacksonville Animal Shelter where authorized personnel will assign a registration number to the animal and shall direct the owner to a licensed veterinarian to cause a computer chip to be implanted in the animal. Documented proof of said implementation must be returned to the Jacksonville Animal Control, which shall maintain a file containing the registration numbers, names of the animals, and the names and addresses of the owners. The owner shall notify Animal Control of any change of address.

This ordinance might not seem so bad on first glimpse because at least those who registered their dogs and otherwise complied got to keep them. However, a Jacksonville newspaper, The Leader, reported that animal control officers started to see an increase in loose pit bulls. This increase was the likely result of owners who dumped dogs as opposed to taking the necessary steps to keep them (similar reports of abandoned pit bulls were also given in Miami-Dade County). If a registered dog is caught running loose and unclaimed, it will have to be moved out of the city and the owner gets a $100 fine. If the owner doesn't claim the dog, perhaps due to lack of cash—which most of us experience from time to time—the dog will be put to sleep. However, unregistered dogs are the most negatively affected according to the code:

5. *Violations*

c)   Any animal seized under the terms and conditions of this Ordinance by Animal Control shall be held by the Department for Three (3) business days for the owner to reclaim the animal. Any such animal shall be retrieved only upon compliance with all provisions of this Ordinance and after payment of a Seizure fee of One Hundred Dollars ($100.00).

The owner must also sign a Statement verifying that the animal will be permanently removed from the City limits within Forty-eight (48) hours.

d)   If any animal seized under the provisions of this Ordinance is not reclaimed within Three (3) business days as prescribed above, said animal shall be euthanized in a humane manner.

ANIMALS

e)   If any animal seized under these provisions is found within the City limits a second time, the owner shall, upon conviction in the Jacksonville District Court, be fined pursuant to JMC § 6.04.120.   Any such animal seized by Animal control a second time shall be euthanized in a humane manner. (Ord. 1312 Sec. 1, 2007)

How do you euthanize an animal in a humane manner? It sounds kind of like, "Well, we're going to put you to sleep now because of what you look like, but we're so very benevolent and enlightened that we'll at least do it humanely." Puhhlease!

Regardless of who makes the decision in these towns/counties about which dogs look enough like the dogs they are banning, there is always the likelihood of error. As The Real Pit Bull Web site notes, "Very few people can accurately identify dog breeds." Even shelter workers, whom you might think would be experts, can make mistakes, especially because they're dealing with so many animals. My Corgi mix Penny was identified as a Jack Russell Terrier mix by the Humane Society shelter workers prior to my adopting her. The county animal shelter didn't even venture a guess as to what type of dog Maggy is. I just gave it my best guess after searching the Internet for pictures of similar dogs.

Looks can be deceiving, but even testing the DNA of dogs can reveal very different breed heritage than what many people would predict based on the dog's actual appearance. I remember reading a Dog Fancy article in my veterinarian's office awhile back. The DNA of various dogs was tested and the results were very surprising. Likewise, an article in The Christian Science Monitor on July 5, 2007 discusses a relatively new breed test that genetically identifies almost 40 AKC-recognized breeds. One couple who had their dog tested found it was mostly Siberian husky. The sign on the cage when they adopted the dog read "spaniel/Plott hound mix."

So, if someone's beloved family pet finds a hole in the gate one day and gets out, and is rightly or wrongly identified as one of the outlawed breeds, that dog might end up put to sleep. Scary! (So scary to me that while I'm researching this part of the book, I actually have a nightmare about a ban being passed in my area and "the law" coming after Barney.)

The site www.pitbullsontheweb.com poses the following scenario in which "law abiding owners, whose dogs love people and have never done anything wrong, can see their homes invaded, often without a search warrant, and their beloved family members dragged away (in front of their children) to be killed."

I think about the elderly, disabled woman I saw in the veterinarian's office. She must depend on that dog for companionship and protection. I pray nobody ever tries to take her dog, but, unfortunately, in my life I've seen firsthand that the law isn't always applied equally or wisely, and, when this happens, the innocent can and do suffer with no recourse.

By the way, Understand-a-bull.com lists states with laws prohibiting municipalities from passing breed specific legislation: California, Colorado, Florida, Illinois, Maine, Minnesota, New Jersey, New York, Oklahoma, Pennsylvania, Texas and Virginia. It's something—a ray of hope or at least a start. But, I notice that some of the states listed on Wikipedia as *having* breed-specific legislation— such as New York— are also on the Understand-a-bull list of states *prohibiting* BSL. Texas has a state level law prohibiting BSL, but also has a local municipality listed as having "unconfirmed" BSL. To help clarify things, I send an email and am told by Understand-a-bull.com site creator Marcy Setter that there are a few ways this can happen:

> "1) BSL was passed within the city prior to the state passing the law. These laws stay in place until they choose to repeal them, once a city repeals BSL they would not be able to pass another BSL law because they would be held to the state law prohibiting it.

> "2) Some states have what is called home rule where cities that meet the state's requirements can pass laws and not abide by state law. The criteria for home rule varies

greatly by state and not all states have such a thing. Colorado for instance has very weak criteria, something like only 2,000 residents, etc.

"3) Then there are the cities that just ignore state law and pass laws until someone challenges them in court or threatens to."

Understand-a-bull lists the 10 worst places to travel with dogs based on breed specific law. Ontario, Canada is listed as the least dog-friendly place because it allows for "confiscation, and destruction of dogs based solely on a dog warden's say so." The top three worst places in the United States are Ohio, Iowa, and (many cities and counties in) Washington. I also asked Setter about whether she has any particular source for keeping up with BSL updates. As I suspected from my own research, there is no one quick way of finding information. Setter said that the lists she posts on her Web site come from checking several pit bull-related and canine legislation forums, media alerts, and emails from people providing updates.

"It is VERY time consuming and impossible to keep completely updated," Setter related, adding that she's developed some methods personally, such as using "confirmed" for cases in which she has seen the law or article and "unconfirmed" if it comes to her through word of mouth. (Montana and Idaho are listed as having "unconfirmed" legislation, for example.) She stresses, "We always say, before moving, contact the city for the most updated information. If the city you're going to isn't listed but a lot of others in the area are, double check with your city."

Good advice, as it's harder to get information on some states and other laws are still coming into existence. For example, no information was available on Understand-a-bull about Minnesota; and North Carolina and South Dakota have areas discussing BSL. To help prevent these laws from spreading, use Web sites, such as Understand-a-bull, to keep apprised of areas discussing possible legislation. This site and a number of others provide advice on how to work to prevent such laws if they are proposed in your area or how to repeal such laws if they are already in existence. Most say it's easier to prevent a law than to have one removed from the books, so staying alert will probably pay off.

By the way, I consider having Barney's DNA tested but decide not to for a number of reasons. For one, I like being able to say with assurance that he's a bully breed mix when people ask me if he's a pit bull. I figure that way most people will react much more favorably to him. Also—after Barney's fight with Casey when I witnessed with my own eyes Barney's refusal to give up—I am pretty well convinced that, if Barney isn't a pit, he can do a damn good impression of one. Also, at this point, I don't really care what a test says. To me he's Barney—a great dog who can always put a smile on my face. (One recent example is when I gave him a taste of a new healthy dog treat I had bought at the grocery store. He didn't like it. But, Drama King that he is, instead of spitting it out, he swung his chunky head from side to side to fling it from his mouth.)

• **Join an online pack.**

Internet user groups can help if you have questions about pit bull ownership or want to communicate with likeminded pit bull lovers. And, believe it or not, there are plenty out there. Under "Yahoo! Pet Groups," there are over 300 such groups. One example is APBT_LOVERS, which was founded in August 2002, and has over 1,250 members.

Groups.yahoo.com/group/dogholocaust is an anti-BSL group.

• Be an official advocate for a bully.

Some rescue groups and shelters are actively working to help change the negative bully breed image. For example: Maddie's Fund is devoted to helping "the nation's most needy dogs and cats." The fund has already awarded grants to organizations addressing the need to find loving homes for bully breeds. For more information, visit www.maddiesfund.org.

• Wear your animal-loving heart on your sleeve, or back, or bumper...

Tee shirts with pro-bully breed messages, as well as pro spay and neuter messages for pets in general, are available from a wide variety of animal-related organizations. This merchandise lets you get pro-animal messages out to others, and often some or all of the money you pay for these shirts and other items goes to an animal-related charity. For instance, working through the Web Site, Cafepress.com, BAD RAP (Bay Area Doglovers Responsible About Pitbulls) sells all sorts of items with positive bully breed messages, including pins, tee shirts, clocks, stickers and posters.

• Babyproof your dog or dogproof your child.

One way to do this is through training. For example, Jennifer Shryock of Cary, N.C., created a "canine re-education course" called Dogs & Storks. An article in the Wall Street Journal on June 2, 2008, relates that this course boasts "35 affiliated trainers in the U.S. and Canada, with hundreds of graduates" who learned how to prepare dogs for the arrival of human babies/children into their lives.

When I visit her blog for more information, I find that, coincidentally, Shryock also adopted a bully breed dog who was a mess physically. The dog, Windsor, is pictured as he is now in his happier days since his rescue from a neglectful owner—an absolutely gorgeous brown and white companion (who actually looks like he could be Barney's relative – if not a brother, than perhaps a close cousin). On a blog, Shryock describes Windsor as "the most wonderful teacher who has continued to educate me and bring so much love." (Again, could be Barney's kin!)

Shryock's Web site is: www.familypaws.com. Among other helpful information, her site contains a section about canines and body language. One warning in this section of the site: When a dog flicks its tongue or turns away, it can indicate stress. As an example, a picture of a happy child hugging a possibly stressed dog shows how easy it is to misinterpret or totally miss a dog's warning signs.

There are DVDs and books available as well on the topic of how to make sure that your dog can co-exist with human infants after being replaced as the "children" in the household. "Childproofing Your Dog: A Complete Guide to Preparing Your Dog for the Children in Your Life," is written by experienced trainers Brian Kilcommons and Sarah Wilson.

Mike Wombacher is the author of a number of books, including, "There's a Baby in the House: Preparing Your Dog for the Arrival of your Child" (which I read when writing my book and recommend as succinct and enlightening). According to an online biography at Amazon.com, the author has been involved with dogs for over 20 years and performed over 15,000 dog behavior consultations. In addition, he has trained dogs for such celebrities as Robin Williams and Sharon Stone.

When I speak to Wombacher during a phone interview, he informs me that he has a lot of experience training pit bulls. Two California rescue groups, including BADRAP (Bay Area Doglovers Responsible About Pit Bulls), refer pit adopters to him. He describes pit bulls as sweet, incredibly intelligent, super fun and real characters.

"But they like to fight, and when they fight, they don't turn off," Wombacher relates, stressing that he is referring to dog-to-dog aggression, not dog-to-human aggression. He emphasizes that because pits are still bred to fight, this pugilistic aspect of their personality should not be overlooked or ignored. On the other hand, he says he has known a lot of pits that have never been in a fight in their lives. In other words, use caution when your pit is around other dogs (similar to what The Real Pit Bull site advised – see Chapter 3). He would have no worries about raising a child around a pit bull if it were a properly trained and socialized animal.

Still, Wombacher's key advice to others about kids/babies and dogs is to never leave any dog alone with a child, as children are less likely to be able to control impulses causing them to behave in ways that annoy or irritate a dog. Equally important, he says, is to start preparing your dog as far in advance as possible when a baby is on the way. Safety issues—such as possessiveness of food or toys, or even pulling on a leash during a walk—can go from harmless to dangerous when a baby arrives. Waiting till baby comes often means dog ends up being booted from the home when new parents are too busy taking care of the new human to be able to deal with a suddenly problematic pooch.

Books designed to help foster a love of canines and/or teach kids how to care for pets have been written for a variety of different age groups. "May I Pet Your Dog?: The How-to Guide for Kids Meeting Dogs (and Dogs Meeting Kids)" (preschool to Grade 2) by Stephanie Calmenson and "Tails Are Not for Pulling (Best Behavior)" (preschool) (winner of the ASPCA Henry Bergh Children's Book Award) by Elizabeth Verdick, are highly rated on Amazon.com. I ordered both for my nephew, Jesse, when he was only 8 months old. Hey, I figure it's never too early to instill a love of animals in a child.

In July, I take Barney to the dog park for the first time. It's a rainy afternoon, which usually means few or no others at the park—a seemingly good way to start off introducing him to being off leash around other dogs he doesn't know. At first, Barney and I are alone in the "big dog" part of the park. A few people are letting their tiny dogs play in the other fenced-in section. Then, a woman brings in a 3-year-old Shnauzer. I explain that this is Barney's first trip and that I have concerns about whether he will get along with new dogs. She is very friendly and understanding. When Barney starts to play with the Shnauzer, I get worried. Barney is too aggressive, practically jumping on top of the dog. Every time the dog gets out from underneath, Barney chases the Schnauzer and moves his larger body back over him. I pull my dog off and try to get him to calm down. His whole body is tense. He's not in attack mode or anything. He is attempting to play— he just doesn't realize his own strength or know to hold back. After a minute or two, I pull the plug, grabbing Barney by the shoulders and putting the leash back on. The woman appears relieved and leaves pretty abruptly with her dog.

Since we're alone again, I let Barney back off leash. I look over and see one lone man and pet in the small dog area. If he had anything against bully breeds, we're sure as hell not doing anything to change that impression for the better.

You can almost hear a "round 2" bell ringing as a woman in her early 20s enters with a 20-pound Cocker Spaniel. The little guy is so cute. This kind of dog always reminds me of a mop—albeit a very adorable mop— because it of its shaggy, long ears. Again, I give the, "I'm working on socializing him," speech as a precaution. The woman doesn't seem too concerned. For maybe 20 seconds everything is peachy as Barney and the adorable, fluffy mop play together. Then, Barney jumps on the dog and bites one of its ears. The woman helps me separate the two—or, more accurately, get my extremely horrifying mass of muscle off of her sweet, floppy ragamuffin. Apologizing profusely, I get Barney's leash on again. After putting him in the car, I walk back into the park to ask the woman if she would like my phone number in case she has to take her dog to the veterinarian.

"He just has a cut on his ear," she tells me. "Don't worry. It'll be fine."

She adds that her dog is always picking fights with other dogs and he gets himself in trouble because he likes to get right in other dogs' faces. If you ask me, she's probably exaggerating her pup's propensity for battle to make me feel better. And—although it doesn't work—it's appreciated.

Back in the car, I decide that the dog park is not the place for Barney. I remember back to various warnings I've read about how pit bulls aren't the dog for people who like to take their dogs to off leash parks. Because Barney is so good with the other dogs (except Casey, of course) and cats at home, I hoped he would be an exception. It would have been advantageous if I could have socialized him as a puppy instead of taking him to the park for the first time when he is already large and strong. Other people are able to bring pit bulls to the dog park without incident. I've seen them with my own eyes. Barney's behavior today also makes it easier to understand how non socialized, un-neutered male dogs without training could pose a threat to other smaller animals. Neutered and smothered with attention, Barney was enough of a challenge.

Like the author/trainer Mike Wombacher pointed out to me when I interviewed him, it's hard for pit bulls, which have been specifically bred for fighting, to ignore their genetic predisposition. Something I stated to Wombacher during the interview comes back to me now. I told him that when I started writing this book I thought my purpose would be to write about how pit bulls are just like any other dog. The more I experience with Barney I have, the more I realize that is not the case.

My journey with Barney thus far has been somewhat amorphous. I think I'm rounding the bend to one conclusion and then along comes some unexpected situation that makes me and my beliefs head in another direction. Today led us in a direction I didn't want to go and I feel kind of bad at the moment.

I wonder what the future will hold for Barney. Certainly not a lot of carefree playing with other dogs as this was his first and, I decide, his last dog park experience.

Then I start to relax. Barney puts his head on my lap while I drive. Now that he feels safe in familiar territory, he's back to being the same sweet, gentle lunkhead I've come to know and love. I pat his head and he slobbers on my lap, which I don't mind because it's not gross—it's just Barney drool.

He's a bright dog but he's not a genius. He was excited and that was reflected in his behavior. Based on what I've seen of Barney since he arrived on my doorstep in January, he's capable of overcoming the odds. There was a point when I didn't even think he'd make it through the day. And another point when I was afraid to let him out of the spare bedroom to be in with the other dogs and cats. But that night he curled up on the couch with three of the cats and slept. The veterinarian believed he might not ever fully recover from his stomach problems. And, now he's as regular as any of the Queen's Corgis.

So the dog park didn't work out. We'll find some other kind of exercise that's better for him.

Besides, my other dogs have their issues that I don't question because they're not surrounded by a breed stigma. Barney doesn't chew books like Maggy did. He doesn't scare vets through fearful body language as Samantha still does. He doesn't guard his food like Libby. He doesn't get too needy for affection like Lilly sometimes will. He isn't, well…actually Penny doesn't have any issues. And, he's not a fence jumper, neighborhood pool invader (I'll explain in the next chapter) like Casey.

Anyway, with time and effort, this dog will probably continue to amaze me. He's not perfect, but he's got a lot going for him. He's brought a lot of laughter and delight to my life. Just the other morning, he was at my feet in the bathroom while I was getting ready for work. I went into the bedroom to get dressed and came back in a new outfit. Instead of remaining seated as he usually does, his ears perked up and he jumped up and did his stretchy thing, where he puts his paws on my stomach. I swear it was the dog version of: "Is that a new outfit? You look nice."

Plus, recently he's been playing with Lilly, my small terrier mix. It's sort of amazing that they're forming a friendship. Also reassuring is that when Barney pushes Lilly too far, she will stand up to him with a warning posture and bark/growl. And Barney backs off without showing the slightest need to assert his dominance.

And so, we head home: a little wiser, a little older, a little more realistic. Oh yeah, and a little wet from drool.

Chapter 9

A lot of my experiences with Barney have made me question how much I actually know about dogs. There are some things, however, I do know for sure that have helped before and after Barney's arrival, and I'd like to share them.

It's simple but true. Dogs who get regular exercise are happy dogs. It helps to find out what a dog likes in order to allow them to expend their energy in the best way possible. Samantha will chase a Frisbee till she can't run anymore, but Casey is not so big on fetching. He usually watches me throw something and then runs off in the other direction. But, he loves to run and to swim. About a month after I moved in to this house, Casey got outside and jumped the fence. He took off to the next door neighbor's house (the ones who later yelled "git" at him repeatedly when he ran in their yard one day). It was dark, maybe about 9:30 p.m. on a weeknight. I hadn't even met them yet and I couldn't see over their fence, but I could hear the grand splash as Casey did one of his enthusiastic running jumps into their in-ground pool. I don't think they were outside, but they *had* to have heard him from inside their home. I've seen Casey do his running leap at the lake—it's like the dog equivalent of a cannonball. He came back soaking wet a few minutes later and the neighbors never said a word to me about it. I seriously hoped that they had a sense of humor, were sound sleepers who went to bed very early, or had extremely short memories.

Maggy just likes to run, whether it be with other dogs, or in circles by herself. She's not much of a swimmer though. She used to make people laugh when I'd bring her to the pond at the local agricultural center (where I stopped going because Casey wanted to chase the occasional car that would drive through—the center is a series of buildings and fields connected with 15-mile-per-hour roads and parking lots). While my other dogs were running in and out of the water, Maggy would stand at the edge and whimper, not sure whether she wanted to go in. She would pat at the water with her paw and bark at the other dogs until she was half submerged, swimming only with her front paws. After she realized they were having too much fun without her, she finally started to do a very tentative doggy paddle close to shore. When she came out, the frame of her body would show because her usually thick and fluffy fur was flat and dripping with water. She'd look like a drowned rat as she ran across the field flipping water in all directions. Maggy is goofy much of the time. My experiences with most spitz dogs is that—while they are ridiculously beautiful—they have lots of personality quirks. I've read that spitz dogs (breeds such as chow chows, Pomeranians and huskies) are the closest dogs genetically to actual wolves. If this is true—contrary to the vicious, cunning characters of fairy tales—wolves might be some zany animals.

Anyway, when my dogs have regular exercise, they're less intense in every way and much more content. It's not even bad behavior that leads a lot of people to turn dogs in to shelters. It's their normal amount of energy that some people are intimidated by, leading to that "I can't handle this dog" mentality.

Besides letting your dog(s) engage in regular activities, be wary of using physical force against a dog under the guise of the dominance theory of training. A number of current books explain this dog training myth in depth. In a nutshell, the whole idea of showing your dog that you are boss through physical aggression—so that he or she will see you as the alpha male of the pack and show you respect—is bunk.

In an actual wolf pack, on which the idea of dominance is based, the alpha male usually gets respect by subtle communications, as opposed to attacking other wolves. Which makes sense because if the dominant male were fighting other wolves all the time the pack would lose cohesiveness. I see this with Casey who is good at getting his point across without any contact with the other dogs. He's used to being the only male dog and the leader that all the other dogs defer to. And, until the fight with Barney, he never used physical aggression. Prior to that, whenever Barney got too close, Casey responded by showing teeth or, if Barney pushed his luck by standing there barking, Casey would lunge forth in warning. But that's as far as he went.

The Monks of New Skete are credited with the dubious distinction of introducing the alpha roll (flipping a dog onto its back and holding it by the throat to show it the human is dominant) into general public discussion. Even they later decided that maybe endorsing this type of training wasn't such a good idea. By then it was too late. The theory had already been adopted by trainers all over the country. A friend of mine told me about a trainer she knows who recommended that she pick her dog up by its ears next time it showed food aggression! Other trainers recommend yanking on a leash. Besides dogs being needlessly physically abused under the guise of "training," some dogs might end up less assured and more aggressive. At the least, it doesn't do much to build trust between a dog and handler. A Web site article by Paul Owens—an author of books on "nonviolent" dog training—beautifully explains the importance of a non aggressive relationship between dog and human:

"Asking your dog to lie down before releasing him to go up the steps or out the door presents terrific everyday training opportunities. So does asking him to sit before being fed, or asking him to jump off the couch so he can be rewarded by getting back on the couch to sit with you. But asking for these behaviors and rewarding your dog is much different than 'showing him who's boss' and forcing him to sit, lie down, and obey you in all things under the threat of punishment.

"So ask yourself why you are teaching your dog to sit, lie down, and come when called. For safety purposes? Ideally, we train our dogs to respond to our signals so we can help them and ourselves be all that we can be. Training stimulates growth and forms a bond between us because it involves communication and interaction. A synergy emerges allowing both our dogs and ourselves to grow and learn in ways that are unique and might otherwise be impossible. I have learned as much, if not more, about patience, honesty, compassion, and congruity—matching my words to my actions, thoughts, and emotions—in the companionship of dogs as I have in any other endeavor. In addition, I believe my dogs have also benefited in ways I can't even imagine."

As Owens' words suggest, friendly repetition is one key to teaching dogs. Like I mentioned earlier, mine behave better when there's a regular routine in the household. They have also learned a lot through simply hearing or seeing something more than once. No tricks, no treats, no punishment. Just repetition. For example, strangers standing nearby are always amazed that when I tell Samantha to "Get in the back seat" of the car as we are leaving the park, she jumps right back there without hesitation. Similarly, when I tell my dogs to "Get down for a minute," when they're on the bed and I'm changing the sheets, they do move to the floor. I never consciously trained them to do this. I can't remember the point when they realized what I wanted them to do following those words. But, I'm sure I said, "Can you get down for a minute?" enough times while simultaneously guiding them off the bed, and now my words are sufficient to make them move.

They all know what "Do you have to go outside?" means as well as other numerous phrases they hear on a daily basis. When I say, "I'm going to take a nap," they clamor for the bedroom door (even Barney, who still sleeps on the couch in the living room—only now instead of being denied bedroom privileges because of stomach issues, it's because I want Casey to still have some territory he doesn't have to share with the "new guy"). They do the same thing when I turn off the television at the end of the night before going to bed.

Being social animals, many dogs also respond well to enthusiastic tones. Phrases such as "good job" or "good work" are rewards that my dogs appreciate hearing almost as much as an edible treat.

Samantha, who has been with me the longest, appears to have the best grasp of what I'm saying. She can even detect by subtle facial expressions whether I'm saying something serious or in jest. As I mentioned earlier, if it's in jest, she'll wag her tail. This dog seriously has a good sense of humor. Maybe I sound a bit like Jane Goodall talking about chimpanzees or something, but, given a chance, dogs can show in all kinds of ways how well they understand us.

Amanda, my friend with two pit bulls, has similar experience with her dogs. In an email, she writes about life with them while her husband is away during the week taking college courses:

"I don't know if all dogs are like this since these are the first inside dogs I have had but my dogs are really smart! I'd like to think it's their breed but they know what you say. Like, in the morning, I'll be getting dressed and I'll say, 'Mommy has to go to work this morning and I'm running a little late so we need to hurry up and go outside and use the bathroom' and they usually do. And then at lunch when I go home to let them out, I always let them out for just a few minutes to use the bathroom and I'll tell them, 'Let's go inside and eat and then I'll bring you back out after lunch' and they always run right back to the door. And then on Fridays, I tell them, 'Daddy's coming home today,' and they'll get all excited. I swear they know what I'm saying. It makes my lonely life a little better, except maybe I'm crazy because I talk to my dogs."

If she's crazy, I'm certifiable because I sing to my dogs too. But I'm sure many people talk to their dogs because dogs truly are so good at responding in various ways. Hopefully, no dog "experts" will come out with the recommendation that we not speak to our dogs. You never know. It's kind of like with babies. Everyone has advice: some of it helpful, some of it ludicrous. I heard on the car radio recently that dogs don't like to be hugged because it makes them feel as though they're being dominated. No doubt there are dogs out there that don't like to be hugged, but mine do. To confirm this, I hugged Samantha when I got home and the other dogs swarmed me for their hugs.

Finally, one of the most important things to remember when you're dealing with a difficult dog (or cat, for that matter)—and this is from someone who has been there multiple times—is that patience is extremely important. Some problems are short-term and typical of bringing an animal into a new environment. Maggy's book chewing was annoying, and definitely didn't make me a popular patron at the local library, but she grew out of it.

That animal 'from hell' today might tomorrow turn out to be the pet that you have no idea how to live without.

Chapter 10:

When writing this book I learned a lot about pit bulls, but I'm still far from being an expert. These are complicated animals, and the way they are viewed in society today is a complex mix of truths, half truths, generalizations, overgeneralizations, exaggerations, rumors, misconceptions, misunderstandings, blatant lies and myths. And these beliefs aren't limited to the Unites States. Breed specific legislation banning pit bulls has been established in various locations around the world. (By the way, in June of this year, the Dutch government announced that its ban on pit bulls, put in place in 1993, will be repealed because no decrease in dog bites had been seen since the ban was instituted. The country plans to start focusing instead on leash laws and owner education programs, according to the Associated Press.)

Since Barney showed up, daily experiences have taught me more about all the dogs who live with me.

So what have I learned?

For one, I am getting a lot better at being in control of the dogs; not for the sake of power, but in order to keep things running peacefully and smoothly. I've never been an imposing person, but I've found that tone of voice and stance needed to get Barney to take me seriously—to see me as dominant without my having to use any physical force.

As I mentioned earlier, I thought when I started writing this book that I would find out pit bulls are just like any other dog. What I've found instead is that they can be great dogs, but I would not recommend that everyone run out and get one. I would not, however, recommend *against* adopting a pittie. I think probably the most successful adopters in many cases would be those who have plenty of time to exercise a dog and to make sure the dog has a place to get such exercise. I also think being a person who doesn't mind a "strong" presence in a pet would help. Those who want a dog that is background noise and doesn't want a "say" in choice of daily activities—well, I'm not sure what kind of dog is needed—but a pit bull is not it.

As for adopting a pit if you have other pets, I'd say to use your best discretion. Plenty of bully breed dogs get along just fine day in and day out with other animals. But Barney doesn't fall into that category when it comes to Casey. Keep in mind that all dogs can exhibit some aggression and that aggression can't always be predicted by a human using human logic.

If you already have a dog that causes any hesitation, err on the side of caution. Never leave that dog alone with another canine or cat. They might be just fine when you're there, but territorial or other squalls that get out of hand quickly can take place when you're not around.

I definitely advise never leaving a young child/toddler/baby alone with ANY dog, no matter how peaceful the relationship has been up to that point between said dog and child/toddler/baby. Of course, I strongly recommend that all people (not just those with dogs) teach their children about coexisting in a world with dogs, such as not touching a dog's food bowl and how to react when a strange dog crosses their path.

It's safest to never assume either way—that is, never assume your pit bull is an angel or a devil. It's probably a dog with all kinds of good traits and some not-so-desirable traits too (actually, kind of sounds like human beings, huh?). By the way, it's almost midnight on a Friday as I type this and Barney is roaming around wanting attention. He starts trying to lick my cat, Stella, who swats him in the face. Discouraged, he moves on to play with Lilly (my small terrier mix). She is warming up to him a little but still gets upset when he plays too rough. So, I end up separating them, as I'm about to do now...

...Okay, I'm back. A potential pit adopter should definitely be aware of the threat of breed specific legislation, which would make life more complicated for anyone who plans to move in the future to an area that might turn out to have BSL.

An adopter should go into the experience knowing they'll need a thick skin for those potential negative comments they might come across when walking their dog in public; and a tolerance for hearing the dog (or the type of dog) they love maligned by the press, television, movies or on the Internet.

On a related note, I work hard to make sure none of my dogs get loose because I don't want them to get lost or hit by a car. With bully breeds there's a whole added element of fear. What if Barney gets out of the yard, and someone sees him and overreacts? It's terrifying to care so much for an animal that others might react toward with hostility. (In July, a highly publicized news story in eastern North Carolina involved police officers shooting a pit bull described by its owner as "so incredibly sweet" outside its home.)

On the flip side, as I remarked in an email to Marcy Setter of Understand-a-Bull—after I emailed her for yet more information about BSL and she promptly responded—there's a group of people with bully breed dogs I'm glad to belong to. They are very friendly, helpful, responsible and dedicated/loyal to their dogs. It's almost like a secret society that should have its own handshake.

Okay, well maybe not that dramatic, but it is a great group and we *do* have shared characteristics—particularly an appreciation for these beautiful and misunderstood animals.

Yes, there are drawbacks to pit bull ownership. But, dogs such as Barney can make those drawbacks seem minute in comparison to the pleasure of their company. If you've never seen a bully breed dog play, you're missing out. When I buy all the dogs their own balls with ropes through them, Barney takes his with him when let outside and practically soars around the backyard. He flips the ball into the sky and then flies up a foot or two after it. His body is acrobatic in its movement; I expect him to do a complete sideways flip in the air. He chews the ball, makes it squeak and then flips it again. His body is like the end of a loose hose with strong water pressure flowing through it; his front half moving one way, his bottom half twisting the other, his tail wagging. What appears to be a grin is spread across his face. How could anyone watch this dog play and not smile?

I can now totally identify with what Vicki Hearne wrote in "Bandit":

"Also, pit bulls are pit bull *terriers*. Even in the most bulldoggy individuals, there will be something—a sprightliness in the stance, some suggestion of the possibilities of tap dancing and vaudeville, some impish gleam in the eye—to suggest the terrier."

When I prepare my dinner in front of him, he sits at my feet and does this thing with his eyes involving blinking repeatedly as if trying to appear adorable and in need of food. I try to resist, but it's impossible not to laugh at this dog with his now pudgy belly sticking out acting as if there's been a terrible kibble shortage.

Life with Barney *would* be A LOT easier if he were my only dog. And, heck no, not a lot of people would make the same choices to share their space with as many animals as I do. But, all things considered, we're a pretty happy pack.

Barney arrived in the winter and by the spring, he was getting huge—prompting me to joke that I might have taken in a bull mastiff mix. I doubt he'll actually get that big, but he is both tall and getting thicker around the middle all the time. In the spring, I bought him a gold collar with rhinestones on it. Once adorned with the collar, he looked like some kind of purebred valued at $1,000. When he played with Libby, his rhinestones flashed as he ducked and weaved. Barney the Crowned Prince. Barney the Rock Star Dog. Then, his neck grew again. Only a couple of weeks later, the collar no longer fit. I bought him collar #3, donating the gold collar to Maggy. Barely two weeks after that, Barney's neck and head grew and I had to buy him collar #4. It's blue and has sea turtles on it in honor of the snapping turtle incident. The veterinary assistant assured me the collar can be loosened if it needs to be. It was the beginning of June and we were at the veterinarian because Barney's stomach was finally stable enough for him to get neutered. I brought him home the same day. The veterinary receptionist told me to make sure he rested for seven days. On day two, with a stomach full of pain medicine and sedative, he slept for maybe an hour during the day and spent the rest of the time trying to play with the other animals.

Now that he's neutered, I'm going to take him for training once a class opens up in the fall. I'm heeding the advice I've heard over and over while researching this book – make sure your bully breed dog is well behaved in public and respects you as the one to listen to (instead of the other way around). Plus, when we go out in public, he gets very excited. On one of his second trips out and about, I took him up to campus with me. A female student we were passing told Barney he was beautiful. After asking, "Does he bite?" and getting a negative response, she spent a few minutes petting him. I was kind of mortified that he jumped up on her with all the grace of a stampeding rhinoceros, but she didn't mind.

A few days later, Barney came with me on a car ride to a fast food drive-through. I ordered an iced tea and had to hold him back because he wanted to give the girl in the window a special greeting.

"Does he bite?" she asked.

"No, he just wants to love everyone," I responded.

"He's gorgeous," she said.

We drove away from the window very proud of ourselves but also in need of a less fulsome way of greeting people.

That same trip, I also brought him back on campus with me. He was, of course, on a leash, but we were walking in one direction and a male student heading toward us made a point of not only *not* passing us, but redirecting his path around a bench to avoid doing so. I think Barney's feelings were hurt. Fortunately, a co-worker came along at the same time and gave Barney a friendly greeting.

Overall, he has a pretty amazing temperament for a dog who had almost starved to death when he showed up at my front door. He was eating dirt to stay alive. I can't even look at the pictures of the condition he was in back then without becoming teary-eyed. Who let him get into that condition?

When you hear about pit bulls in organized fights, who's behind the whole thing? Bully breeds might strike fear in the minds of many. But, from what I've seen, human beings do more harm to animals than the reverse. And usually the worst offenders are those who are ignorant because these are the people who are mostly easily led by fear.

Thank God dogs aren't very good at holding grudges against humans. If they were, all breeds might start displaying the outrageously aggressive behavior pitties are accused of. Instead, dogs are often patient teachers. All the dogs I've adopted have brought something new and special into my life.

Penny taught me that dogs really do experience complex emotions, including being grateful. She didn't stop licking my hand for days after I adopted her. It was as if she couldn't believe she was in a real home with someone to look out for her and she wanted to make sure I didn't disappear. I always think of Penny as "the good girl." If she were a human, I could picture her in pigtails, keeping up a straight A average at school and rarely ever misbehaving. Her first owners turned her in because their neighbor convinced them to—the owners weren't paying attention to even her most basic needs most of the time. It was as if she was determined to show that, as soon as she was given a chance, she could be the best dog ever.

Maggy showed me that it's possible to overcome fear and—in spite of how scarred you've become—you can find that inner goofball and the strength to let it come back to the surface. I don't think Maggy had a good start in life at all. When I brought her home, it took weeks before I could even pet her without her ducking her head as if she thought she was going to get hit. Then, one day, I called her name and she came flying across the room, jumped up on my lap and started licking my face. It was the beginning of a beautiful friendship.

Lilly helped me realize that even if you're small, you can still earn respect from the big dogs by standing your ground. I also learned that beagles do make noises like Snoopy. Even beagle mixes.

Casey—who was a real nightmare the first year he lived with me but went through training and is now mild mannered and well behaved—showed me that not giving up can yield amazing results.

Samantha has been a loyal companion for the past 10 years. She got me through a really bad breakup in my last semester of grad school. Her needing to be walked and exercised motivated me to leave the house when all I wanted to do was curl up in bed and cry. And on those occasions when I did curl up and cry, she was there voluntarily to snuggle up next to me—even though, prior to that time, she mostly preferred the floor to the bed.

As for Libby…well, I believe that Libby is still teaching me whatever it is that the universe wants me to learn from her. Ever since her veterinary appointment, I've been working with her almost daily for about 10 minutes at a time (I guess neither of us have particularly long attention spans). I've almost cured her of jumping up on me, and, hopefully, on other people. Mostly, we work on her sitting on command and "hold"-ing (staying in a sit until I tell her it's okay to get back "up"). Even though I was skeptical of the advice from the veterinary assistant, it does work. Libby seems to be more grounded and responds much more quickly to me when I reprimand her. This change has made it possible, so far, for me to head her off when she's getting too aggressive in her demeanor with the other dogs BEFORE she jumps on them. I don't know if this is a cure. I'm finished with predictions except for this one—dogs will never cease to surprise me. I might never be able to take her back to the dog park, and I need to watch her constantly, but her progress is heartening and we still haven't gone back for doggy meds to control her aggression.

And this book covers a small amount of what I've learned from Barney.

Around the time I'm working on the end of this book, I've been watching "The Dog Whisperer" during a marathon on National Geographic network. I'm happy to report a lot of the dogs on that show make my dogs (even on their worst days) look like cream puffs.

And, for anyone wondering, I love my cats too, but it's a whole different type of relationship and would require a completely different book to describe the role they play in my life. Truly, they too are loved and bring something special to the household.

It was mostly during the spring semester of 2008 that I wrote this book. During that semester, I went through a couple of pretty rough months involving a problem student's ongoing disruptive behavior in class. During that time, I went through all the administrative steps faculty have to go through to make sure the university doesn't violate the rights of while still disciplining that student.

And, as is often the case whenever something goes wrong and you're already in a bad mood, things start to spiral. *Do I really want to do this job anymore?* and *What is the point of trying to teach when students don't want to learn?* were some of the questions repeatedly running through my mind. That then set off an existential crisis. *Why are we here? Why am I here? Am I making any difference in the world at all?*

One evening in the midst of everything, I took a book and went out onto the porch with the dogs. I was looking out over the back fence. Maggy jumped up on the bench on one side of me, Barney on the other. While the others ran around, we three sat and looked at the trees in the backyard where the woods start behind my house. My dogs were such pleasant yet silent companions that my spirits lifted. It didn't solve my problems. I knew they'd still be waiting for me at work, along with heartburn, migraines and tension.

Just like they always do, my furry, four-legged friends provided a moment of relief. Peace and happiness for a few, fleeting minutes in the midst of disarray. And a little tilt upward in my confidence that things were going to be okay.

It was yet one more reason to love them, and one more missing piece of the puzzle.

One more way of explaining the magic of dogs.

Postscript:

I didn't hear anything back from the county commissioner
to whom I sent a letter and a packet of information about
establishing an anti-tethering law. Nothing. Not even a
letter stating that he received my letter.

After I found an explanation of the process on the
Internet, I was going to contact the secretary and request to
have a discussion of such a law added to the agenda of the
next Board of Commissioners meeting. Then, I had a
reconciliation of sorts with my neighbor. After she came
back on my property once again—this time mowing even
though I had mowed the day before—I went out to hang up
a Private Property sign, and she came over with her
husband. Long story short, we all agreed that there were a
lot of misunderstandings between them and I. I still don't
agree with a hundred percent of what they were saying, but
would rather have a truce than continue to feud.

Unfortunately, although I didn't want to bring their
dogs into it, the subject did come up. They said my dogs'
barking one night last summer had kept them awake. (My
dogs were outside that night because the air conditioner
was broken and it was stifling in the house. Apparently, she
was starting a new job the next day, was already having
trouble sleeping and one of my dogs kept barking.) I said I
was somewhat surprised that she would complain about my
dogs since they're usually inside at night, unlike her dogs.
Her husband then mentioned that he was going to "get rid
of" the hunting dogs soon because of lack of time to hunt. I
stressed that his dogs didn't bother me; I didn't want them
to become an issue and his "get rid of" phrase sounded kind
of ominous.

The next day I was outside mowing in the back
yard. I noticed that only one dog was back there, and I

started to feel sick to my stomach. What if those dogs were gone because of what I had said? And what would become of them? Would he take them into the woods and let them go? To the pound to be put down? I couldn't stop staring at all the empty pens that looked like a third world prison. The ground was mud and dirt with holes dug by the dogs here and there. The smell of feces was evident. The plastic barrels they sleep in were askew. I had to wonder if maybe they weren't better off wherever they were now. Ironically, the only dog still back there was the one kept tethered outside of the pens. If an anti-tethering law suddenly came through around here, would that dog "disappear" too? The next day, I looked out the window and saw that all the dogs were back. I guess my neighbor must have suddenly found time to take them hunting or something after all. Strangely, I felt relief at seeing them back.

There was no question in my mind that I was going to follow through until a law was passed. But, it suddenly seemed prudent to wait until I could be sure of what the next step should be—I didn't want to push the neighbors into hastily *getting rid of* the dogs. In situations such as this, timing can be everything.

By July, as I finished the rough draft of this book, the neighbors still had all four dogs but had moved the one dog that was always tethered into one of the metal pens. Two of the dogs have about a 15-by-10-foot pen they share and the other two that are back there have their own individual pens of about the same size. The tops have canvasses over them offering at least some protection from the North Carolina sun.

The second summer semester—which had been eating up a lot of my time through teaching and grading— was coming to an end; after which I knew I'd have much more time to pursue getting the anti-tethering law passed without having to have another showdown with my neighbors.

So, as I conclude this book, I'm also focusing back on getting the tethering law in Pitt County. There are still plenty of other dogs out there who are tethered that can hopefully be helped.

2680036

Made in the USA